D0721375

Partisan Warfare *1941-45*

Text by

NIGEL THOMAS and PETER ABBOTT

Colour plates by

MIKE CHAPPELL

OSPREY PUBLISHING LONDON

Published in 1983 by
Osprey Publishing Ltd
Member company of the George Philip Group
12–14 Long Acre, London WC2E 9LP
© Copyright 1983 Osprey Publishing Ltd
Reprinted September 1983

British Library Cataloguing in Publication Data

Thomas, N
    Partisan warfare 1941–45.—
    (Men-at-Arms series; 142)
    1. War   2. Guerilla warfare
    I. Title   II. Abbot, P   III. Series
    335′.02184   UZ40

ISBN 0-85045-513-8

Filmset in Great Britain
Printed in Hong Kong

Author's Note.

The partisan war was one of immense size and complexity and we have limited ourselves, perhaps artificially, to Eastern Europe and the Balkans. Even so, in a compact study such as this, it is impossible to do more than sketch in the outlines of the struggle and indicate something of the nature of the forces involved.

These were not restricted to German Army and Waffen-SS versus Communist Partisans, and we have tried to bring out the importance of the Nationalist guerillas and the little-known auxiliary security forces who bore much of the brunt of the conflict. If the latter seem over-represented in our plates it is because they, being localised and extremely heterogenous, require a more detailed treatment than the partisan movements, which were more standardised in uniforms and organisation.

We have hardly been able to touch on the complexities of German policy in the Occupied Territories. Those interested should read Norman Rich's *Hitler's War Aims*. The best simple account of the partisan war in Russia is Martin Cooper's *The Phantom War*; its bibliography acknowledges its debt to the work of Armstrong, Howell and Dallin among others. There is as yet no equivalent account for the Balkans, but the recently reprinted *German Operations in the Balkans* (originally one of the US Army's World War II German Military Studies) provides a valuable summary from the German point of view.

Again, we would like to acknowledge the generous help provided by others, notably P. Buss MA; Dr. S. M. Fostun (Association of Ukrainian Former Combatants in Great Britain); Franklyn G. Prieskop; Pierre C. T. Verheye; Dr. F. Herrmann; G. Curry; J. Allan; Henry L. de Zeng IV; H. Rüütel; P. Pavasović (Yugoslav Ex-Combatants' Association); H. Gaidis; Father A. Nadson (Byelorussian National Library); and Brian L. Davis.

Introduction

During 1941 the Germans occupied first Greece and Yugoslavia, then enormous areas of European Russia. The front line troops soon moved on, but the struggle was far from over, for bands of resistance fighters sprang up and waged a ceaseless war against the occupation forces until their final withdrawal.

There were several reasons why resistance in Eastern Europe took on the character of guerilla warfare earlier and to a greater extent than in the West. To begin with, the terrain was more favourable. The Balkans were mountainous, and Russia had great expanses of forest and swamp, all excellent hiding places for guerillas. Then again, the Germans released many of their Greek, Yugoslav and Russian minority prisoners, and failed to round up a great many other stragglers, so there were more able-bodied men available—men whose cultures and recent history offered many examples of irregular warfare. Finally, German occupation policy was far harsher in the East than in the West, especially in the Slav areas, so that even those who had welcomed them as liberators soon came to see them as oppressors.

The term 'partisan' is associated with Communist-led bands, and it is true that Communists provided many of the most determined resistance fighters. In Russia they were inevitably the most fanatical defenders of the Soviet regime. In the Balkans the Party had long been harried by the pre-war police, and its members were skilled in the techniques of evasion. After Germany attacked Russia their duty was clear: to hinder the German war effort by any means possible. Their influence was enhanced by the fact that their ideology had not been contaminated by association with the pre-war regimes: moreover, it cut across regional differences.

However, there were also non-Communist resistance groups which were nationalist and broadly constitutionalist. They tended to hate the Communists as much as they did the Germans, and in some areas a complicated three-sided war de-

SS-Sturmscharführer Ackermann of the Sicherheitsdienst. Note the use of Police shoulderstraps of rank, in silver and black mixed cord on a green underlay, which dates this photograph to 1942-45. This most senior of non-commissioned ranks was authorised—at the same time as the change from W-SS to Police shoulderstraps—to wear an officer's-quality service cap with silver chin-cords; note that the *Waffenfarbe* piping is in the white of the Allgemeine-SS rather than the 'toxic green' officially used by the SD. This branch of the SS often displayed anomalies of uniform and insignia, and the open tunic collar worn with a shirt-collar and tie by this NCO is a further reminder of the liberties taken by this basically un-military organisation. Photos sometimes show NCOs wearing tunic collars complete with silver *Tresse* opened in this way. (Courtesy Brian L. Davis)

veloped, with the nationalists fighting both the occupation troops and the partisans. Often little divided such groups, ideologically, from the collaborationist 'Home Guard' and militia forces, and as the war went on and the partisans increased in strength, they sometimes found themselves tempted into unofficial alliances with the Axis troops.

German policy towards the occupied territories was a mixture of dogma and expediency. The Slavic East was to be occupied permanently. The 'Germanic' areas were incorporated directly into the Reich, and the rest placed under a form of protectorate administration (the 'General-gouvernement' of Poland and the 'Reichs-kommissariate' of 'Ostland' and 'Ukraine'). The Army administered the areas adjacent to the front. Originally envisaged as a temporary measure, this arrangement lasted throughout the war, and in fact replaced civil administration as the Germans retreated westwards. The Rumanians were given the area of Transnistria, and they and the Hungarians and Slovaks provided security units for areas nominally under German control[1].

[1]See MAA 131, *Germany's Eastern Front Allies 1941–45.*

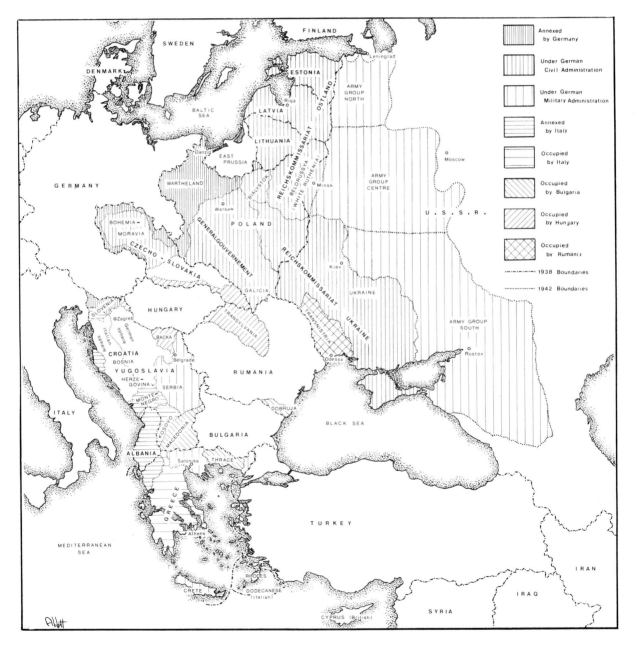

The Germans made few concessions to the desire of anti-Soviet groups such as the Balts, Ukrainians, Caucasians, Byelorussians and some Great Russians to have their own forces. They reluctantly permitted them to serve as auxiliaries in the German Army, Police and SS; but it was not until 1944, when they had been forced out of the occupied territories, that nominally independent Russian and Ukrainian armies came into existence.

The situation in the Balkans was even more complex. Hitler's original idea was to let Italy police the region, and initially the Italians stationed some 30 divisions there, compared with the Germans' six. The German-controlled territories were placed under military government. Thrace and Macedonia were handed over to the Bulgarians, who also provided an occupation corps to help the Germans in Serbia. Collaborationist governments were set up in Greece, Albania and Serbia and permitted their own limited security forces. Croatia was given its 'independence' and encouraged to raise its own armed forces and party militia, in the hope that they could maintain order in its territories without help.

Ukrainian villagers welcome German invaders with genuine delight in 1941. The German failure properly to harness anti-Soviet feeling among many minority populations, in refusing to hold out any political rewards for collaboration, had incalculable consequences. (Imperial War Museum)

Unfortunately for the Germans, these measures proved ineffective. They were able to crush a Serbian revolt in 1941, but not to stamp out the rival Chetnik and Partisan movements. The Allies' invasion of Italy in 1943 brought them within striking distance of the Balkans, and the subsequent Italian collapse meant that the Germans had to disarm the sizeable Italian garrisons and replace them with additional occupation troops which they could scarcely spare. Inevitably, greater reliance had to be placed on the remaining collaborationist forces, but in the event these ill-assorted levies were to prove of little help when the Russians swept into the Balkans in 1944.

The security forces were heterogeneous in the extreme. The foundation was provided by indigenous police forces who remained in being and co-operated to a greater or lesser extent with the occupation authorities. These were supplemented

A sergeant (right) and private of the Polish Home Army during the 1944 Warsaw Uprising. Both wear virtually regulation 1939 Army field-uniform.

by a miscellaneous collection of home defence units called into being by the unsettled conditions, and encouraged by the Germans because they resisted the exactions of the partisan bands. Many were composed of 'Volksdeutsche'—there were colonies of these ethnic Germans scattered throughout the Balkans and Eastern Europe; others of minorities like the Vlachs in Northern Greece, or the Tartars of the Crimean peninsula. Above these were the collaborationist gendarmeries such as the Serbian State Guard, puppet and allied police and security forces, and the various German forces.

These last presented a particularly complicated picture. In theory the distinction between military and civil rule was clear, with Himmler's SS and Police supreme in the former and the military forces controlling the latter. In practice the situation was more complex. Although the local Higher SS and Police Leaders were responsible for Police security within the protectorates, there were also Army commanders who were responsible for military security there, and who often took control of anti-partisan operations. Within the areas under Army administration the Army had overall responsibility for security; but ultimate authority was divided between the local Army commanders and the Quartermaster-General, the first answering to the Army High Command (OKH), the latter, like the other Rear Area commanders, to Hitler's rival Armed Forces High Command (OKW). Moreover, SS and Police units were present in large numbers in the operational areas. In theory they were subordinate to the Army, but this was not always true in practice. These arrangements were simplified in 1942, when Himmler was made responsible for anti-partisan operations within the protectorates and the Chief of the (Army) General Staff for those within the operational zone—measures which were followed by the appointment of SS General von dem Bach-Zelewski as Co-ordinator of Anti-Partisan Operations in the East. Nevertheless division of authority, with all its inevitable duplication, remained a characteristic of German security policy. This was equally true in the Balkans, where the Army concluded sourly that the system of parallel Army and SS commands had led to considerable confusion and wasted effort.

In theory, the SS were intended as an élite gendarmerie to police the conquered territories (and, of course, to carry out the deportations and executions dictated by Nazi racial policies). They did play this role in Poland, but by the time of 'Barbarossa' most of the German rank and file had been absorbed by the Waffen-SS, so that apart from the infamous Einsatzgruppen only a couple of brigades and cavalry regiments remained for security duties. These security formations were subsequently diluted with Baltic and Ukrainian recruits. Nevertheless, the SS continued to provide the overall direction for the security effort in the rear areas through the Higher SS and Police Leaders and their SD (SS Security) staffs.

The paramilitary German Police took over the mobile gendarmerie role. Each Higher SS and Police Leader had at least one regiment at his disposal, including those in Greece and Serbia. However, the Police, too, began to be diluted with local recruits. In 1943 they were divided into the German 'SS Police' and indigenous 'Police Rifles' regiments. The territories to be controlled, however, were so vast that the Police needed additional support. During the early days of the German occupation the surviving local police forces were supplemented by local militias and home defence units sponsored by the temporary Army administrations. In Russia, many of these scattered units were consolidated into an auxiliary police force known as the Schutzmannschaften ('Schuma'), composed mainly of Balts, Cossacks and Ukrainians, and divided into 'Front' and 'Guard' units. In the Balkans Serbian, Croatian and Montenegrin Police Volunteer Regiments were formed from Volksdeutsche Hilfspolizei.

Although the SS and Police operated within Army-administered areas, the Army had its own security formations. Initially, Russia was allocated no more than nine Security Divisions, each made up of one line and one Landesschützen regiment, with a mobile Police battalion and a handful of artillery. These under-strength and under-equipped units were quite inadequate for their task, especially as they soon lost their best combat elements to the front, and from late 1942 Reserve and Field Training Divisions were stationed throughout the occupied territories to reinforce them. The Army's need for manpower was also met by the creation of Eastern volunteer units as a kind of Army equivalent to the Schuma. At first prohibited by Hitler and established clandestinely, these 'Eastern Troops' (Osttruppen) soon received reluctant recognition, and came to form a major element of the Security Divisions[1].

For the Balkans the Army raised a handful of 'Light Divisions' in the '700' series, two-regiment formations comprising over-age men. They were equally unsuitable for their task, and as the partisan war increased in intensity they had to be supplemented by a motley collection of reinforcements, with an occasional front-line unit such as 1st Mountain Division posted in to provide a striking force for major sweeps.

The other Axis powers either annexed their new territories outright or adopted a straightforward policy of military government, garrisoning their areas with reserve or security divisions. These were generally similar to their line divisions, but with reduced artillery and transport, and formed from second-line personnel. Indeed, all the occupation troops were poorly equipped with obsolete or booty weapons, and, in Russia particularly, they often found that the partisans possessed better small arms.

The partisan war undoubtedly caused the Germans and their allies serious concern, but not to the point of forcing them to divert a large number of troops from the front. It has been pointed out, for instance, that the total of German troops and SS men on security duty in the East never even

An officer of the Polish 'People's Army' (second left) wearing the 1939 officer's tunic and collar-patches, pictured with Soviet troops, late 1944.

approached the number stationed in Norway, and seldom exceeded 200,000, few of whom were combat-worthy. They were too few to stamp out the partisans, but enough to safeguard the essential communications network. As far as the Balkans are concerned, it is often claimed that by 1944 the partisans were pinning down over 20 German divisions: in fact many of these were there to counter the threat of an Allied landing, and most were only second-line formations. Notwithstanding partisan claims to the contrary, it is doubtful whether their activities affected the course of any major campaign.

The real significance of the struggle lay in its long-term political effects. The success of the partisan movements in Albania and Yugoslavia in particular led to the establishment of Communist regimes there after the war. Perhaps 'after the war' needs some qualification, however, since nationalist partisans were to go on fighting the Soviets long after the Germans had surrendered in May 1945, and in this sense the partisan war can be said to have continued well into the 1950s.

* * *

[1]See MAA 147, *Foreign Volunteers of the Wehrmacht 1939–45*, November 1983.

Poland

The Germans split up conquered Poland in 1939. Large areas were incorporated directly into the Reich, others into the 'Reichskommissariate' of 'Ostland' and 'Ukraine', and the rump was administered as the 'Generalgouvernement'. German policy was uncompromising. A brutal racial war was to be waged to Germanise the incorporated areas as quickly as possible, while the Poles themselves were to be treated as slaves. Hitler refused to deviate from this policy even when the Russians were poised to overrun Poland in 1944 and his lieutenants were begging him to capitalise on the Poles' anti-Russian feelings. There were to be no organised Polish units in the Wehrmacht.

Soviet Partisans on parade. Many carry the ubiquitous 1941 model PPSh sub-machine gun. The man in the peaked cap and leather coat (both symbols of Soviet authority) is probably an NKVD man acting as commander or commissar.

This repressive policy required a strong security presence. Initially the SS and SD operated in force, but after they had moved on to Russia in 1941, security was shouldered by 12 German Police Regts. ('Krakau', 'Radom', 'Lublin', 'Warschau', 4, 10 to 12, and 22 to 25). The Polish Police were retained but closely supervised. Following the principle of 'divide and rule', a separate Ukrainian-Galician police force was raised for the Province of Galicia. Twelve Schuma Bns. (201 to 212) were raised, but most were Ukrainian-Galician, and only one, the 202nd, was specifically described as 'Polish'. There was inevitably a strong military presence too: in all the Germans kept between 400,000 and 600,000 police and troops in Poland.

Nevertheless the Poles resisted from the start. An underground Association for Armed Struggle was formed in late 1939, becoming the AK (Armia Krajowa, or 'Home Army') in 1942. Although drawn from a range of pre-war political parties and

politically far from unified, the AK was broadly nationalist and constitutionalist, and recognised the authority of the Polish government-in-exile in London. Unfortunately, the right-wing NSZ ('National Armed Forces') stood aloof, as did the Gwardia Ludowa ('People's Guards'), a left-wing organisation set up in 1942.

The AK was by far the biggest of the resistance groups, with a maximum strength of 400,000, but at first it held back from outright guerilla warfare in order not to provoke German reprisals. This gave the smaller GL a propaganda advantage. In practice the reprisals occurred anyway, and during the winter of 1942–43 the AK went into action and succeeded in forcing the Germans to halt their programme of forced evictions.

The AK had plans for both limited risings (codenamed 'Tempest') and a general revolt. 'Tempest' began in eastern Poland, where the AK's 3rd, 9th and 27th Divisions (named after pre-war formations) tried to drive out the Germans ahead of the advancing Russians. The latter, who favoured the Communist-dominated Lublin government, simply arrested the AK officers and drafted their men into the new Russian-sponsored Polish army. 'Tempest' continued, however, with the ill-fated Warsaw Rising in August 1944. The Russians proved unable or unwilling to advance to the aid of the capital, and the Germans were able to destroy the AK there. It never recovered from this defeat, and was formally dissolved in January 1945. Bands of AK and NSZ irreconcilables, Ukrainain partisans, deserters and ordinary brigands remained at large, but effectively Polish resistance had been overwhelmed at the moment it came out into the open: not so much by the Germans as by its ostensible allies the Russians.

For space reasons we have limited description of the Polish resistance to these few lines, since its background and course are more fully summarised by Steven Zaloga in MAA 117, *The Polish Army 1939–45.*

* * *

The commander (left) and adjutant of Estonian Police Battalion 35. Both wear German Police insignia on distinctively non-regulation tunics. Note the Estonian national arm-shield. (Henry Rüütel)

Russia

At dawn on 22 June 1941 3,400,000 German troops hurled themselves against the 4,700,000-strong Red Army which, although numerically superior, was unable to offer effective resistance. As the Wehrmacht advanced inexorably eastwards it placed occupied territory under military government, with the intention of turning it over progressively to civilian government after it had been pacified. Hitler intended to occupy all of European Russia, and to organise it into four Reichskommissariate, named Ostland (Estonia, Latvia, Lithuania and Byelorussia), Ukraine (Southern Russia), Moskau (Northern Russia), and Kaukasus (Transcaucasia). These would be under civilian administration, defended by an Army garrison deployed along the Ural mountain range.

Events, however, took a different course. By December 1941 the merciless Russian winter and a revitalised Red Army had combined to halt the German advance just short of Moscow, and at the end of 1942 the Stalingrad débâcle prevented more than a partial occupation of Transcaucasia. Ostland and Ukraine were established as Reichs-

Members of an Estonian Police Battalion, wearing the M1936 German Police tunic not normally worn in the field, Estonian arm-shields and the M1936 Estonian Army cap-badge. Left foreground is a Russian orphan adopted as unit mascot. (Henry Rüütel)

kommissariate, but only in part, while the rest of occupied Russia remained under military government. The Wehrmacht resigned itself to defending its gains against the external pressure of the Red Army, and the internal distraction of Soviet partisans.

Anticipating a swift and crushing victory, the Germans had not planned an army of occupation for Russia, and when it became clear that all first-line troops would be required for a protracted war at the front, it combed its reserves for occupation troops. From March 1941 middle-aged reservists were formed into nine, later 14, Security Divisions (52, 201, 203, 207, 213, 221, 281, 285, 286, 390, 391, 403, 444 and 454). Understrength and equipped only with light weapons, they guarded lines of communication against partisans. Each division eventually included two security regiments, an 'Eastern Battalion' of Russian auxiliaries, and a battalion of German Police. In the western Ukraine, Hungary operated an Occupation Corps of five, later 14, divisions, with Rumanians and Slovaks in the South[1].

Predictably, these scratch units could not cope with the partisans alone, and in 1942 they were joined by five Reserve Divisions (141, 143, 147, 151 and 153), containing raw recruits who fought as

[1]See MAA 131, *Germany's Eastern Front Allies 1941–45*

they trained. Later seven Field Training Divisions (52, 154, 381, 382, 388, 390 and 391) arrived, comprising trained recruits; and even eighteen-year-old youths performing six months' pre-military labour service in the Reicharbeitsdienst could be required to fight when necessary.

In June 1942 German Police Battalions were organised into motorised Police Regiments (after February 1943 called SS-Police Regiments), each regiment having three or four battalions, with signals, armoured car and anti-tank companies. Fourteen Police Regiments (2, 6, 9 to 11, 13 to 17, 22, 24, 26 and 38) served in Russia, as did seven Police Rifle Regiments (31, 33 to 38), which were mixed German-Russian units.

Heydrich's Security Service (SD) provided four Action Groups (Einsatzgruppen A to D), each about 1,000 men strong, formed from SD cadres assisted by Police, Russian auxiliaries and Waffen-SS personnel, and divided into Einsatzkommandos. They achieved a fearsome notoriety, and certainly bolstered partisan ranks by their ideological mass murders of Jews, Soviet officials and other 'undesirables'.

Although the Soviet Union had inherited a vigorous guerilla tradition dating back at least to the Napoleonic Wars, Stalin had forbidden any planning of partisan warfare, believing both that this would be defeatist, and that it might encourage internal rebellion. The State Security Service, the notorious NKVD, had, however, formed company-sized Destruction Battalions before the war, but they had only trained as guard units. On 3 July 1941, eleven days after the German attack, Stalin broadcast a call for national resistance, ordering the formation of partisan units (Otryadi) in all occupied areas. An Otryad had 200 to 1,000 men and women, comprising Red Army stragglers, escaped prisoners-of-war, NKVD troops, Communist activists and Komsomol (State Youth Organization) cadres, but few peasants or workers. Communist Party members, facing certain death at the hands of the Einsatzgruppen, provided up to 40 per cent of partisans, but could not prevent the Red Army gaining control of the movement.

Stalin's territorial system, which insisted that Otryadi be established uniformly throughout occupied territory regardless of necessity, proved too inflexible. For instance, in the Baltic States anti-

Soviet nationalism was almost universal, and Soviet agents soon abandoned them as hopeless; while in the Ukraine, nationalism, a lack of Army stragglers, and open countryside with little cover, combined to virtually rule out partisan operations. Central Russia, the Leningrad area and especially Byelorussia, with their relatively sympathetic populations, thick forests and impenetrable marshes, were ideal, and about 80 per cent of the active partisans operated there. Even so, they were at first no more than a minor irritant to the Germans. By December 1941 many units, even the supposedly fanatical NKVD Destruction Battalions, had been destroyed or had voluntarily disbanded; and only some 30,000 partisans remained, badly led and equipped, fighting ineffectively, and at the mercy of the Russian winter.

The year 1942 brought a dramatic improvement. Regular troops infiltrated through the lines on foot or by parachute, combining with increased numbers of stragglers to expand the demoralised Otryadi. Arms were flown in or rescued from secret Red Army dumps; the German anti-partisan troops were themselves too badly equipped to yield much booty. Partisan raids became more effective, and numbers of Germany's Axis allies, especially the Slovaks, were persuaded to desert to the partisans. By spring there were three types of unit operating: the best was the 'Military' Otryad, with regular Army officers and personnel. Next came the 'Civil' or 'Irregular' Otryad, led by commissars and Party members—dedicated but militarily inexperienced. Finally, the 'Self-Protection' Otryad provided rudimentary village defence. Nevertheless, most

A 'Virsnieka Vietnieks' (Warrant Officer II) of a Latvian Schuma Battalion, wearing Latvian Army uniform and national arm-shield, being decorated along with SS officers for bravery in the field.

units were only third-rate militia, and no match for the Wehrmacht.

In May 1942 Moscow established the Central Staff of the Partisan Movement, at Army Headquarters but under close Party supervision. This controlled Partisan Staffs attached to the Army Groups ('Fronts'), which in turn supervised Territorial Commands in occupied territory, each Command containing a number of Brigades. The unnumbered, named brigade, about 1,000 strong, became the main tactical unit; usually it comprised the commander, Party commissar, headquarters company (with NKVD security section), a 400-man support company (usually the original Ot-

ryad), and three 100-man rifle companies, each with two or three platoons. Peasants were openly and if necessary forcibly conscripted, and eventually made up 60 per cent of partisans, the remainder being mainly Army personnel. By December 1942 there were 130,000 partisans controlling large areas in the German rear, well armed with machine guns, anti-tank weapons, some abandoned Soviet tanks, and, in the Bryansk region, even a few aircraft. The main operational area, however, remained Central Russia, with only token forces in the West or South. In August 1942 some 'mobile brigades' tried to carry the war to the Ukraine, but soon withdrew.

By 1943 regional administration was operating in 'liberated zones', and the distinction between military and civil units had largely disappeared.

The funeral of a Latvian Schuma soldier, 1943. His comrades wear Latvian Army uniform with the M1934 Czech Army helmet supplied as booty by the Germans.

A Lithuanian Schuma battalion building earthworks. Note the typical blend of national Lithuanian and German-introduced black uniforms.

Former collaborators, usually Ukrainians, joined the partisans under an amnesty that was usually honoured, and by 1944 they comprised 20 per cent of units. Improved communications with Moscow permitted joint operations with the Red Air Force. By January 1944 there were 200,000 partisans, but their separate identity was at an end. The Central Staff was abolished, and as the Red Army advanced westwards, and the partisans fought more aggressively, their brigades were absorbed into Army units. This was an appropriate anti-climax to a movement which never matched the Yugoslav partisans in popular appeal or military value.

Anti-Partisan Forces

From June 1941, much to the bewilderment of the Germans, large numbers of Soviet citizens attached themselves to the invading forces, either as 'Hiwis' (Hilfswillige, or unarmed auxiliaries), or as discip-

lined fighting units, as in the Baltic and Ukraine. When the front stabilised, and the inadequacy of German manpower to police the occupied areas was revealed, these volunteers were cautiously enlisted as armed auxiliaries. In the Military Administration Zone the German Army organised recruitment, and in the civil Reichskommissariate it was organised by Himmler's SS (embracing the Waffen-SS, SD and German Police), although there was overlapping and duplication where both zones met. From the vast supply of ex-Soviet manpower the Army recruited 'Eastern Battalions' (later re-organised as Russian and Ukrainian 'Armies of Liberation'), Cossack divisions and 'Eastern Legions', while the Waffen-SS established five combat divisions[1]. (Although the latter were

[1]See MAA 34, *The Waffen-SS (Revised Edition)*

13

sometimes used against partisans, they were eventually, if not originally, conceived as front-line troops, and thus fall outside the scope of this study.)

The Military Administration Zone was divided longitudinally into the Combat Area, Army and Army Group Rear Areas. In the Army Rear Areas 14 Security Battalions (Sicherungsabteilungen), mainly Estonians, but with some Latvians, Lithuanians, Russians and Karelian Finns, served within German Security Divisions. In October 1942 these became either Eastern Battalions or Auxiliary Police ('Schuma'). The Army Group Rear Area was patrolled by Army Security Divisions, German Police and Schuma. Although the Army formed five Estonian mobile Protection Battalions (Schutzmannschaft-Abteilungen), these too were re-mustered as Auxiliary Police by mid-1942. This left only local home guard companies and battalions under Army, as opposed to SS and Police,

control; these were known in Army Group 'Nord' areas as Local Combat Units (Einwohnerkampfverbände); in 'Mitte' as Order Service (Ordnungsdienst); and in 'Süd' as Auxiliary Guards (Hilfswachmannschaften). All these troops repaid their occupiers for petty favours and protection by performing useful services, often of a kind to attract the interest of post-war atrocity investigations. So too did such local strongmen and gangsters as Bronislav Kaminsky, who governed (in a rather medieval sense) Lokot Province in Central Russia from 1942–44 on behalf of the Germans, and kept it free of partisans. But all their willing co-operation and military potential was wasted by the stubborn German refusal to offer them even the prospect of political autonomy after the war.

In November 1941 all locally-raised police in the two Reichskommissariate were organised into 'Auxiliary Units of the German Police' (Schutzmannschaft der Ordnungspolizei), usually abbreviated as Schuma. Volunteers were usually former soldiers and policemen. Many from the

A Lithuanian Schuma Field Battalion, wearing a mixture of uniforms. Some wear the black Schuma side-cap, but most have retained the former Lithuanian Army peaked cap.

Baltic states of Estonia, Latvia and Lithuania had served in their national police and armed forces before June 1940, and their dedication earned preferential treatment from the Germans. The Schuma was divided into four branches. The normal police (Schutzmannschaft-Einzeldienst) undertook duties in town and countryside. The Schuma Battalions (Schutzmannschafts-Bataillone) were organised for anti-partisan duties. Each battalion had a staff and four 124-man companies, each with one machine gun platoon and three infantry platoons; the nominal total of 501 men was usually swollen in practice to up to 700. There were Frontline, Guard, Engineer, Construction and Replacement Battalions, deployed in the Reichskommissariate and along the entire length of the Army and Army Group Rear Areas. Baltic units had a Baltic commander and two German Police liaison officers, but Byelorussian and Ukrainian battalions each had a German commander and adjutant and 31 other Germans. Of the other two branches, the Auxiliary Fire Police (Feuerschutzmannschaft) contained existing volunteer and professional fire-brigades, while the Reserve Auxiliary Police (Hilfsschutzmannschaft) guarded prisoner-of-war camps and carried out labour duties. The notorious SD also had some Schuma forces (Schutzmannschaft der Sicherheitspolizei), but few details are available about them. Finally, various home guard organisations (Selbstschutz) functioned throughout the territory.

In **Estonia** 26 Schuma Bns. (29 to 45, 50, and 286 to 293) were formed, operating as far south as the Ukraine, and also in Byelorussia. In May 1943 they were officially re-designated 'Estonian Police Battalions' and issued German Police uniforms. In April 1944 all Estonian Schuma became 'Estonian Police' in recognition of their reliable record. Schuma Bns. were re-formed into the 1st Estonian Police Regt. (286, 288, 291 and 292 Bns.) and Estonian Frontier Guard Regts. (Police) 1 to 6, each with three or four battalions. For home guard and anti-partisan duties in Estonia the pre-1940

Soldiers of the Ukrainian Insurgent Army celebrate Easter 1944 in the forest. Most wear Soviet or Polish uniforms, and carry captured Soviet PPSh sub-machine guns.

Civil Guard (Eesti Kaitseliit) was re-organised into 13 regions and a railway region. Re-designated Self-Defence Corps (Omakaitse), they wore modified Estonian Army or Civil Guard uniforms; and in September 1944, after the fall of Estonia, the remnants were re-formed as the 'Fellin', 'Pernau' and 'Kivi' Regts.

Latvian forces developed along similar lines. Members of the former Civil Guard (Aiszargi) were incorporated into Latvian Self-Defence units. An estimated 15,000 men served in 41 Schuma Bns. (16 to 28, 266–270, 271 twice, 272 to 278, 279 twice, 280 to 282, 311 to 313, and 316 to 322), fighting partisans and Red Army at Leningrad, and in Byelorussia and Ukraine. In January 1943 four battalions (16, 19, 21 and 24) were retitled as the Latvian Legion and transferred to the SS. From May 1943 Schuma Bns. were re-designated Latvian Police Bns., wearing German Police uniforms; and all Latvian Police Bns. and SS units were collectively termed the Latvian Legion, with the SS expanding its numbers at the expense of the Police. In August 1943 the 1st Latvian Police Regt. (276, 278, 279 and 312 Bns). was formed, followed in February 1944 by the 2nd (22, 25, 313 and 316 Bns.) and 3rd (317, 318 and 321 Bns.), and by Latvian Frontier Guard Regts. (Police) 1 to 6. In April, just before the Soviet re-invasion, all Latvian

Schuma became Latvian Police, and four new Latgalian Schuma Bns. (325 to 328) were established, soon becoming German Army Labour Units.

Although the **Lithuanians** were as solidly anti-Soviet as their Baltic neighbours, they were almost as firmly anti-German. The Germans had such difficulty recruiting Lithuanians (there were only five Lithuanian battalions in the German Army, and no SS units) that they eventually declared them racially inferior and unfit to serve Germany. Nevertheless 13,000 Lithuanians were prepared to join 23 Schuma Bns. ('Lietuva', 1 to 15, and 251 to 257), recruited from pre-1940 police and army; while former Civil Guard (Siauliai) personnel made up the Lithuanian Self-Defence Bns. The Schuma Bns. were well up to the high Baltic standard, fighting partisans in Byelorussia and the Ukraine, with even a battalion in Italy and one in Yugoslavia. In May 1943 they were re-designated Lithuanian Police Bns., serving in German Police uniforms; and in April 1944 all Schuma were renamed Lithuanian Police.

Nationalist consciousness in **Byelorussia** was weaker than in the Baltic or Ukraine, and only 11 Schuma Bns. were established (45 to 49, 60, 64 to 67, and 69), only three of which were mobile 'Front-Battalions'. But even with massive Baltic Schuma reinforcements they could not contain the partisans, and after the Soviet re-invasion in July 1944 they were disbanded or incorporated in the 30th SS-Division. The Byelorussian Self-Defence Corps (Belaruskaya Samaachova, sometimes incorrectly called 'BNS') was formed in late 1941, attaining nine battalions; and in January 1944 it was re-designated Byelorussian Home Guard (Belaruskaya Krayovaya Abarona—'BKA'). In March general mobilisation was optimistically proclaimed, but the BKA probably never exceeded six battalions. After July 1944 Byelorussians were serving in six Army Engineer Bns. (1, 2, 6, 7, 9, and 11—probably ex-BKA), a BKA 'Cadre Bn.' in Berlin, and the mysterious BKA 'Dalvits' guerilla battalion, which sent infiltrators behind Soviet lines.

Ukrainians joined German-sponsored forces in large numbers, and in late 1942 some 70,000 were in the Schuma. About 35,000 served in 71 Schuma Bns. (51, 53 to 57, 61 to 63, 101 to 111, 113 to 126, 129 to 131, 134 to 140, and 143 to 169), which were raised at different times for anti-partisan duties, and included some Cossack, cavalry and artillery units. Home Guards were designated as the Ukrainian National Self-Defence Force (UNS), with up to 180,000 men. In May 1944, when the Red Army had overrun Ukraine, the much-depleted UNS was renamed Ukrainian Self-Defence Legion before its final disbandment in November. The few remaining Schuma units mostly joined the 30th SS-Division. In the Crimea in early 1942 the SD organised 3,000 Crimean Tartars into eight highly effective Tartar Self-Defence Companies for anti-partisan operations on the peninsula.

Nationalist Partisans

Although many Soviet citizens fought for Germany, only a small minority were pro-German. Most were passionately nationalistic and vehemently anti-Communist, seeing a German victory as the only possibility—albeit a slim one—of regaining or finding independence. Other groups of nationalists, however, believed that this goal was only attainable through a separate partisan struggle. Although independent of both Germans and Soviets, the nationalist partisans sympathised with their countrymen in the German forces, from whom they often obtained weapons and supplies; and occasionally they mounted joint operations against their common enemy, the Soviet partisans.

The Ukrainian Insurgent Army (Ukraïns'ka Povstans'ka Armiia) was established in early 1944 from nationalist elements carrying on the tradition of the Ukrainian National Republic annexed by Soviet Russia in 1921. Commanded by Maj.Gen. Taras Chuprynka, it claimed 80,000 men, although probably only 20–30,000 were active guerilas. It held territory as far east as the River Dniepr, but was most successful in North-Western Ukraine, where it co-operated with Hungarian occupation forces, much to the annoyance of the Germans; and in Galicia (in the Polish Generalgouvernement). In May 1943 the UPA ambushed and killed Viktor Lutze, commander of the German SA; and in July 1944 it rescued Ukrainians in the 14th SS-Division from encirclement at Brody. Originally the UPA was organised in infantry, cavalry and artillery battalions divided into companies, but in 1944 it established four operational commands: North (North-Western Ukraine); West (Galicia); South (South-Western Ukraine) and East (Central Ukraine). After the German retreat of May 1944 the UPA, its ranks expanded by ex-UNS personnel, Schuma, and Eastern Bn. deserters including non-Ukrainians, faced the Soviets alone. In 1947 troops of its West Command fought their way into the American Zone of Austria; but by 1950 the UPA had finally been crushed.

The Byelorussian National Guerillas (Belaruskaya Narodnaya Partizanka) were too weak for effective operations, but the Baltic states had had thriving guerilla movements since the Soviet occupation of June 1940. Estonia had 50,000 'Brethren of the Forest', Latvia about 60,000 guerillas, and the 'Lithuanian Activist Front' 120,000. They attacked retreating Soviet forces in June 1941 but, becoming disillusioned with the Germans, attacked them in turn. In 1944 the old Soviet enemy returned, and the guerillas continued their increasingly hopeless struggle until, with the defeat of the last Lithuanian partisans in 1952, all organised Baltic resistance ceased.

Yugoslavia

Just before dawn on 6 April 1941 German mechanised forces, supported by Italian and Hungarian troops, attacked Yugoslavia. After 12 days Belgrade fell, and the young King Petar II fled to British-controlled Egypt, where he tried in vain to organise a viable Free Yugoslav Army. With 28 infantry

Members of a Dalmatian Partisan Battalion in 1941. Note the Italian and Royal Yugoslav uniform items, the early-pattern rank insignia, and the red stars, some with the Commissar's hammer and sickle.

Tito confers with his Staff, 1944. On 29 November 1943 he received the unique rank of 'Marshal of Yugoslavia', with its distinctive collar, cap and sleeve insignia.

divisions the Royal Yugoslav Army should have been formidable; but hardy infantry, thinly deployed and lacking modern equipment, were no match for the Axis. In the North dissident Croat units refused to fight, and only in Montenegro did the Yugoslavs manage a successful counter-attack.

Hitler dismembered Yugoslavia as he had Czechoslovakia and Poland. Chief beneficiary was the Independent State of Croatia (abbreviated 'NDH'), which promptly annexed Bosnia and Herzegovina. In Serbia Gen. Nedić set up a puppet government, while the detached Serbian Banát was ruled by local ethnic Germans. Germany directly annexed Central Slovenia, Hungary the Bačka and some frontier districts, and the Bulgarians occupied Eastern Macedonia. Italy annexed Western Slovenia and Dalmatia, set up a puppet state in Montenegro, and added Serbian Kosovo to its Albanian possession. Eastern Croatia and Serbia were controlled by the 55th Corps of the German 12th Army, with four second-line infantry divisions, the 704th, 714th, 717th and 718th (in April 1943 redesignated 104th, 114th, 117th and 118th 'Jäger' Divisions), lacking motorisation and logistical support, their primary task was to safeguard rail communications with Greece. However, the main burden of occupation fell to the Italian 2nd and 9th Armies, with 16 divisions and 15 Blackshirt Legions, based in Western Yugoslavia.

In July 1941 demobilized Yugoslav troops and Communist activists in Montenegro rose up against the Italian occupiers. The revolt spread to Slovenia, Bosnia and then Serbia, where the Communist leader, Josip Broz, nicknamed 'Tito', ordered a general uprising. He formed 8,000 men into ten 'detachments' (Odredi), each Odred being equipped with Yugoslav or captured rifles and light machine guns, and overseen by a political commissar. Soon a huge area south of Belgrade was controlled by Tito's 'Partisans', co-operating with nationalist 'Chetniks' in a short-lived alliance. Tito now felt confident enough to set up a Supreme Command, dividing Yugoslavia into Operational Zones; but in September the Germans counterattacked. They threatened to execute one hundred hostages for every German soldier killed, and sent in four more infantry divisions and a Panzer Brigade. By December they had crushed the revolt. Tito retreated with nine detachments to the comparative safety of Italian-occupied Eastern Bosnia, where he joined local partisans to make Bosnia his base for future operations. He realised that the centuries-old Balkan tradition of guerilla warfare against their former Turkish masters, the cohesive discipline of the Communist cause, and the mountainous forested terrain, all combined to favour mobile hit-and-run tactics. Clearly Odredi with local loyalties were not suitable, and so he formed his 1,000-strong élite bodyguard, the 1st Proletarian Brigade, with three battalions each 300 to 400 strong.

In mid-January 1942 large German and Croat forces attacked Tito's headquarters, but he escaped southwards with his brigade to the Jahorina Mountains, waiting out the end of the offensive in early February. In March he formed the 2nd Proletarian Bde. and three territorial brigades. Tito's policy of equal treatment for all Yugoslav nationalities and religious faiths provided a vast fund of goodwill and, more importantly, new recruits. Odredi sprang up almost everywhere, and most towns contained an underground Partisan[1] network; but in spite of urgent pleas, the Soviet Union provided no more than moral support.

In March 1942 a new enemy offensive was launched, but Tito broke through the encirclement and reached Partisan allies in Montenegro. Thus reinforced, he headed back northwards, and by August had formed a new liberated area in Central and Western Bosnia. In November he captured

[1]In the Yugoslavian context we use 'Partisan' as the proper title of a specific organisation, rather than 'partisan' as a general term.

Bihać in Northern Bosnia, where he formed a Partisan Government, the Anti-Fascist Council for the National Liberation of Yugoslavia. His forces, now about 150,000 strong, were designated the Yugoslav National Liberation Army (AVNOJ), and re-organised as two Army Corps, with eight 3,500-strong 'divisions': the élite 1st Proletarian (ex-Brigade), 2nd Proletarian, and 3rd to 8th Montenegrin or Bosnian Divisions. A division had three infantry brigades and an artillery brigade, equipped with captured rifles, LMGs, anti-tank guns and field artillery. There were some mounted units and ex-Italian light tanks, as well as 36 Independent Bdes., 79 Odredi, 70 Battalions and 15 Companies.

In January 1943 Axis troops, including the Yugoslav and ethnic German 7th SS-Division 'Prinz Eugen', the 369th (Croat Legion) Division, and the Italian 5th Corps attacked Bihać, nicknamed 'Titoland'. Tito retreated in good order to Central Bosnia with civilians and wounded, and in February counter-attacked, sending his élite 1st to 3rd Divs. against Italian garrisons in the Neretva Valley. The Italians fell back, but German reinforcements compelled Tito to make a daring crossing of the Neretva River; he established a strong bridgehead in adjacent Chetnik territory, before pursuing the demoralised Chetniks southwards into Montenegro. Now the Western Allies belatedly recognised Tito's achievements and began to airlift to the Partisans the much-needed supplies which had previously gone to the suspect Chetnik forces.

In May 1943 Axis troops, reinforced by élite German 'Brandenburg' commandos and the 1st Mountain Division, and the 61st and 62nd Bulgarian Infantry Regts. from Serbia, surrounded Tito at Mount Durmitor in Montenegro. With difficulty and at heavy cost, Tito escaped back to Eastern Bosnia, where he dispersed his units throughout Yugoslavia. Then, in September 1943 the Italian Army declared an armistice. Italian troops were disarmed, and vast stores of weapons were seized by the Partisans. 'Garibaldi Brigades' were even formed from pro-Tito Italians; and 18,000 Yugoslav troops interned in Italy returned via Bari, now an Allied port supplying Tito, to make up five new 'Overseas Brigades'. Tito's cause prospered in Croatia and Slovenia too, but not yet in Bulgarian Macedonia.

With about half of Yugoslavia liberated, the Partisans numbered 250,000; but the struggle was far from over, for German forces, now designated 2nd Panzer Army, had increased to 13 divisions, including the new 1st Cossack Division. In late October, 5th SS-Mountain Corps ('Prinz Eugen' and 'Handschar' Divs.) attacked Partisans in Eastern Bosnia. Tito's forces survived, but with 11,000 losses. Then the Germans recaptured the Dalmatian island of Korčula, inflicting heavy losses on its defenders, who included two inexperienced Overseas Brigades, and severed the Allied supply line.

By early 1944 the German forces, which now contained some unreliable Eastern Battalions from Russia, were on the defensive. In a final desperate attempt to crush the Partisans, the 2nd Panzer Army attacked 'Titoland' in May. SS parachute and glider troops destroyed Tito's headquarters at Dvar, but Tito escaped to the island of Vis, where he re-established himself with Allied help. His troops now numbered 390,000 men in 14 Corps,

NCOs of the Yugoslav National Liberation Army pose in the field in 1944. The improved uniformity, morale and soldierly bearing is evident by comparison with the 1941 photograph.

This carefully posing Chetnik wears the traditional Chetnik headgear, an Italian tropical uniform (even down to Saharan sand-shoes), and proudly displays his captured German MP40 sub-machine gun. (P. Pavasović)

Kosta Pecanać controlled 8,000 rival Chetniks in Macedonia. Mihailović's Chetniks had mobile (active) and territorial companies, formed into battalions and brigades led by civilians styled 'chieftain' (vojvoda) or by Army officers. Some 10,000 Chetniks fought alongside the Partisans in July 1941, and by 1943 there were 30,000 mobile troops. After November 1941 Partisan-Chetnik co-operation deteriorated into armed hostility; for Mihailović, now Minister of War to the Yugoslav government-in-exile, and receiving Allied aid, saw in Tito a deadly rival, and Communism as anathema to his Serbian nationalism. After January 1943 his troops were re-designated 'Yugoslav Army of the Homeland', fighting Germans, Italians, Croats and Partisans alike.

Throughout 1942 Chetnik fortunes steadily improved. In January 1943 they were re-organised, and based on a three-man 'trojka' cell. Between 15 and 30 Trojke formed a company, three companies a battalion, three battalions a brigade, three to five brigades a 'corps', named after a local river or mountain and often only 2,500 strong. Troops were under ten Area Commands—Serbia (Corps 1 to 37); Stari Ras (38 and 39); Montenegro-Sandjak (40 to 45); east Bosnia-Herzegovina (46 to 54); Western Bosnia (55 to 57); Dalmatia & Coast (58 to 63); Slovenia-Istria (64 to 67): Southern Serbia (i.e. Macedonia) (68); Bačka-Baranja; Srem. Mobile forces were extracted from these units and designated 'Flying Brigades' and 'Shock Corps'.

With early 1943 came disaster. The Chetniks were badly mauled by Tito at the Neretva River, and retreated from Bosnia and Montenegro into Serbia to defend the Chetnik heartland. Meanwhile Allied aid was switched to the Partisans, whom King Petar now recognised. In March 1944 Mihailović re-formed his corps into 'Groups of Corps' 1 to 12, and 'Groups of Shock Corps'. The élite 4th Group of Shock Corps, with 9,000 men, defended South-West Serbia, but after initial success was forced back. The arrival of Soviet troops compelled a dispirited Mihailović, now totally isolated, to retreat in October with his depleted forces to take refuge in the Bosnian mountains. His hostility to the Partisans had led his movement along a dangerous path, beginning with a simple disagreement over immediate objectives, but leading in many cases to outright collaboration with

with Divisions numbered 1 to 39. In September he formed 1st Army (1st Proletarian Corps, Danube Corps) which, with 13th and 14th Serbian Corps, liberated Serbia, linked up with Soviet forces advancing from Rumania, and in October 1944 helped take Belgrade. Ultimate victory was now assured.

The Chetniks
From the beginning Tito's claim to lead Yugoslav resistance was challenged by Col. Dragoljub ('Draža') Mihailović, who formed in mid-1941 his mainly Serbian 'Chetnik Detachments of the Yugoslav Army' ('chetnik' is the traditional Serbian name for guerilla) on Ravna Gora Mountain in Western Serbia, although until March 1943

Axis forces against the Partisans. This had robbed the Chetniks of their credibility, both at home and with the Allies.

Croatia

On 10 April 1941, four days after the Axis invasion of Yugoslavia, the Croatian Ustasha Party leader (Poglavnik), Ante Pavelić, left political exile in Italy and declared the 'Independent State of Croatia' in Zagreb. His policies were virulently Catholic, nationalistic and anti-Serb, even though the immediate annexation of Bosnia and Herzegovina yielded Croatia large Moslem and Orthodox Serb minorities.

The Croatian Army (Hrvatsko Domobranstvo) had a I Corps (Zagreb), II Corps (Brod) and III Corps (Sarajevo), with infantry divisions numbered 1 to 5, each with three three-battalion regiments (1 to 15). There were also four engineer battalions, twelve artillery 'battalions' (each with only four 105mm howitzers), a cavalry regiment, logistical services and some armoured cars, a total of 55,000 men. Italian interference and a chronic shortage of professional officers and NCOs greatly prejudiced its combat value. However, the fanatical Ustasha Militia, organised in five—later 15—700-man battalions, two railway security battalions, and the élite Black Legion and Poglavnik Bodyguard Bn. (later Bde.), fought with a merciless tenacity which impressed and appalled friend and foe alike. An air force was formed, but the Italians vetoed a sea-going navy. Four Gendarmerie regiments (6,000 men) controlled 7,500 civilian militiamen, whilst the German-speaking minority maintained one railway security and three Jäger (rifle) battalions in the Army, and an independent four-battalion 'Einsatzstaffel' dressed in quasi-SS uniform. The Wehrmacht recruited the 369th Legion Infantry Regt. (lost at Stalingrad), and Naval and Air Force Legions, while the Italians sent a 1,200-man 'Croat Legion' to Russia, and organised a 20,000-strong paramilitary 'Voluntary Anti-Communist Militia' (MVAC) to fight partisans.

In May 1941 the Croatian Army was engaged in Eastern Bosnia and Herzegovina, against Serbs driven to desperation by Ustasha terror. In January 1942 it forced the Partisans in Eastern Bosnia back into Montenegro, but could not prevent their subsequent advance into Western Bosnia. Clearly conventional infantry divisions were too cumbersome, and so in September 1942 four specially-designed mountain brigades (1st to 4th) were formed; each had two regiments totalling four 1,000-man battalions, mounted and MG companies, a two-gun artillery group, 16 light and 16 heavy machine guns, and six mortars. Two volunteer regiments, a mobile Gendarmerie Bde. and an Ustasha Defensive Bde. were also established; but by November 1942 the Partisans had occupied Northern Bosnia, and the Croats could only hold main towns and communications routes, abandoning the countryside.

During 1943 four Jäger Bdes. (5th to 8th) were set up, each with four 500-man battalions in two regiments and an artillery group, equipped for hilly terrain, while the Ustasha battalions were re-

The Croatian Armed Forces Commander, Field Marshal Slavko vitez Kwaternik, greeting German officials. He carries a ceremonial axe, the Croatian equivalent of the Field Marshal's baton. (F. Herrmann)

21

A major of Croatian Army General Staff embraces a rather reluctant corporal of a Croatian Legion Division, who has just been awarded the Croatian Bravery Medal. The corporal wears regulation German Army uniform, and would have a Croatian national arm-shield. (F. Herrmann)

2nd Ustasha Corps: 1st, 17th (combining 12th and 14th), 18th Ustasha Assault Divs.
3rd Ustasha Corps: 3rd, 7th, 8th, 9th Divs.
4th Ustasha Corps: 4th, 6th, 15th Divs.
5th Ustasha Corps: 10th, 11th, 13th Divs.
16th Div. (formerly 1st Garrison Div.)

Serbia

In Serbia Gen. Milan Nedić, a well-respected former Yugoslav Defence Minister, wanted to minimise the horrors of the Axis occupation and, as a Serbian nationalist and fervent anti-Communist, sympathised with Mihailović and hated Tito. He formed a 17,000-strong Serbian State Guard, divided into City Police, Rural Police, Fire Service and plain-clothes Village Guards, equipped with small-arms (which they often passed on to Chetniks). The Germans condemned the Guard as unreliable; and in October 1944 Nedić's organisation, now only 5,000 strong, and the Serbian Frontier Guard, once 6,000 men, joined Mihailović in Bosnia as the Chetnik '1st Serbian Shock Corps'.

In September 1941 the Serbian Fascist Dimitrije Ljotić formed a Serbian Volunteer Command, after September 1942 re-designated Serbian Volunteer Corps. It grew from twelve companies (odredi) in 1941 to 7,000 men in early 1944, in five regiments numbered 1st to 5th and an artillery battalion, under Gen. Konstantin Mušicki. Considered by the Germans to be the only efficient Serbian force against Partisans and Chetniks, it transferred in October 1944 to Slovenia, where the Waffen-SS absorbed it. Also in September 1941, Czarist émigrés in Serbia formed the Russian Defence Corps (Russisches Schutzkorps) with an authorised strength of 3,000. By September 1944 the Corps, organised in five three-battalion regiments (1st to 5th), mainly infantry, with some cavalry and a Cossack battalion, was 11,197 strong. Of low combat value, it was relegated to guard duties.

In the Banát an ethnic-German home guard (Heimwehr) was formed, and from June 1942 Auxiliary Police regiments (1st to 3rd) and battalions (1st to 10th) for service in Serbia. Many Banát Germans joined the 7th SS-Division 'Prinz Eugen'. In Montenegro the Italians failed to exploit native nationalism. Some local police units were formed, but the Montenegrins remained staunchly

organised into eight four-battalion brigades (1st to 8th). The SS established a multi-national 'German-Croatian Gendarmerie' with 15,000 men in 30 battalions, and later a Gendarmerie Div. to guard railways. The German Army sent home three Croatian Legion Divisions—369th, 373rd ('Tiger') and 392nd ('Blue'), while the Waffen-SS formed the 7th 'Prinz Eugen' Mountain Div. (absorbing the Einsatzstaffel), and two ill-fated Bosnian Moslem Divisions—'Handschar' and 'Kama'. After the Italian Armistice the Croatian Navy was expanded, but the loss of even an unreliable ally further weakened the Croatian state.

By 1944 Pavelić was almost totally reliant on his Ustasha units, now 100,000 strong, formed in Brigades 1 to 20, Recruit Training Brigades 21 to 24, three divisions, two railway brigades, one defensive brigade and the new Mobile Brigade. There were also the 33,000 men of the Legion Divisions; and the Croatian Army had 90,000 men, though only 20,000 were combat troops, organised in three mountain, four Jäger and eight static garrison brigades, and the 1st Recruit Training Division. In December 1944 the Army was put under Ustasha control, and Army and Ustasha brigades were combined in 17 divisions as follows (correct as in April 1945):

1st Poglavnik Bodyguard Corps: 1st Ustasha Assault, 2nd Ustasha, 5th Ustasha Divs.

pro-Tito or pro-Mihailović, and anti-Italian. In 1944 the Germans formed a plain-clothes Montenegrin Volunteer Corps with 5,649 men in three regiments, but it proved unreliable and in December joined Mihailović in Bosnia. In the Sandjak region (Western Serbia and Northern Montenegro), the Italians had formed in 1942 a 'Moslem Legion' to fight guerillas, but by 1943 it had disintegrated.

In April 1941 the newly formed Bulgarian 5th Army (1st Cavalry Bde.; 14th, 15th and initially 6th Divs.) occupied most of Yugoslav Macedonia. The territory was formally annexed in May, and Bulgaria policed it with such efficiency and brutality that no significant Partisan units emerged until 1944. In January 1942, responding to German demands for reinforcements, the 1st Army (7th, 9th, 21st Divs.) occupied almost all Serbia, and from mid-1943, now with the 22nd, 24th, 25th and 27th Divs., it opposed Partisan advances into Western Serbia. Meanwhile in summer 1942 Germany had to intervene in Italian-occupied West Macedonia, claimed by Bulgaria, to halt armed clashes between her allies.

Unwilling to fight the Soviet Union, Bulgaria changed sides in September 1944 and placed her 450,000 troops under Soviet command. The Germans reacted swiftly and advanced into Serbia and Macedonia. The Bulgarian 1st Army was easily disarmed, but the 5th Army (14th, 15th, 27th Divs.) offered stubborn but short-lived resistance.

The Croatian 'Poglavnik', Pavelić, congratulates members of an Ustasha Militia field battalion. All wear Italian Army uniform with Ustasha insignia. The officer (seventh right) wears his rank badge on the side of his cap.

Slovenia

From spring 1942 the Italians organised indigenous MVAC forces in Western Slovenia. Called 'White Guards' by Tito, they consisted of 6,500 Village Guards for static defence; and the Ljubljana police—called 'The Legion of Death'—which was well-equipped and mobile, to react aggressively to Partisan attacks. Slovene Chetniks and their 'Slovene Alliance' allies (called 'Blue Guards') were virtually annihilated in September 1943 by the Partisans. After the Italian Armistice the Germans re-organised the MVACs into the Slovene Home Guard (Slovenski Domobranci), 10,000 to 15,000 men under the former Yugoslav general Leon Rupnik, while Slovenes in the Trieste region of Italy were formed in December 1943 into the 'Slovene Guards of the Littoral'. In Central Slovenia in April 1941 the German stormtroopers (SA) formed a Defence Force (Wehrmannschaft) from local Germans, to fight Slovene Partisans. Organised in 'Action Companies', these troops, which eventually numbered 66,566, were well-equipped with automatic weapons and even artillery, and dressed in the brown SA uniform.

After the fall of Belgrade in October 1944 the Soviet 3rd Ukrainian Front headed for Hungary. Meanwhile three Bulgarian Armies—1st (1st, 2nd,

Two Bosnian infantrymen in the Croatian Army, displaying shirt-sleeve order and field-dress. Note the scarlet fezzes with Croatian cap-badge, the modified brown Royal Yugoslav uniform with crimson infantry collar-patches. (F. Herrmann)

11th Divs.), 2nd (1st People's Liberation, 4th, 6th, 9th, 12th Divs.), and 4th (5th, 7th Divs.)—re-occupied Eastern Serbia and Macedonia, but could not prevent German troops escaping from Greece to form a defensive line along the Bosnian border. The Partisans now formed a formidable conventional army for the final offensive—800,000 men in the 1st to 4th Armies, comprising the 1st to 53rd Divisions organised in 1st to 17th Corps.

In March 1945 it began. While 4th Army advanced along the coast, 1st and 2nd Armies moved through Central Yugoslavia, and 3rd Army skirted the Hungarian border with the Soviets, and a new Bulgarian 1st Army (3rd, 8th, 10th, 11th, 12th, 16th Divs). By mid-May the war was over. Croatian troops, Russian Schutzkorps and the Slovene 'Army' (formerly Home Guard) entered Austria, while the Serbian Volunteer Corps, some Chetniks and State Guards reached Italy. All surrendered to the British, and most were re-patriated to Tito's Yugoslavia, to face imprisonment or death. Finally, Mihailović's capture in March 1946 removed Tito's last rival from the scene.

Greece

In 1939 Greece was a deeply divided country. The king had been exiled in 1923 and had not returned until 1935. In the following year Gen. Metaxas had imposed a military dictatorship. The country remained divided between the right wing royalists and the more radical republicans, with a small but well-organised Communist Party which had been forced underground by Metaxas' police.

The Italian invasion of 1940 produced a spon-taneous surge of national feeling which temporarily united the country behind the regime. Even so, many officers of known republican views stayed unemployed. In the aftermath of defeat the old political divisions re-asserted themselves. The king left the country to head a government-in-exile, but the Free Greek forces in the Middle East remained split between royalists and republicans, and this led to a serious mutiny in 1944.

Political divisions re-asserted themselves within Greece, too. Initially, at least, the German ap-proach was conciliatory. They placed Greece under military rather than civil (i.e. Nazi) adminis-tration, released many prisoners-of-war, and tried to work through a Greek caretaker government which attracted the support of many of the more conservative elements within the country. Unfor-tunately for the Germans, they could only afford to garrison Salonika, Athens, Crete and some areas adjacent to Turkey. They handed over Thrace to the Bulgarians, and the remainder to the despised Italians. This aroused Greek resentment. The Germans were also unable to replace Greece's blocked food imports, and the population suffered considerable hardship as a result. Inevitably, many young Greeks followed the long-standing local tradition and took to the mountains. Inevitably, too, the resulting partisan movement reflected the political divisions within the country.

There were two main resistance organisations. The left-wing guerillas joined ELAS (the National Popular Liberation Army), which became the largest of the guerilla forces and the only one to operate throughout the whole of the country. It grew rapidly, and by late 1944 had formed ten 'divisions' (1st Thessaly, 2nd Attica, 3rd Pelepon-nese, 6th Macedonia, 8th Epirus, 9th, 10th and

1: Leutnant, Galician Police; Poland, 1942
2: Wachtmeister, German Schutzpolizei Battalion, 1942
3: SS-Untersturmführer, SD-Einsatzgruppe; Russia, 1941

A

1: Virsserzants, Latvian 'Schuma', 1941
2: Korporal, Ukrainian 'Schuma', 1942
3: Korporal, Ukrainian 'Schuma' Battalion, 1943

B

1: Partisan, Polish People's Army, 1944
2: Russian partisan, 1942
3: Partisan, Ukrainian Insurgent Army, 1943

C

1: Satnik, Ustasha 'Black Legion'; Croatia, 1942
2: Visji Narednik, Slovene Home Guard, 1944
3: Narednik, Croatian Army infantry, 1943

D

1: Kapetan I Klase, Serbian State Guard, 1941
2: Kaplar, Serbian Volunteer Corps, 1942
3: Kapitan, Russian Defence Corps; Yugoslavia, 1942

1: Albanian partisan, 1944
2: Chetnik officer; Yugoslavia, 1943
3: Kapetan, Yugoslav National Liberation Army, 1944

F

1: Podofitser, Bulgarian Army infantry, 1941
2: Ushtar, Albanian Rifles, Italian Army, 1942
3: Podporuchik, Bulgarian Army cavalry, 1942

G

1: Ypostratigos, Greek Security
   Battalions, 1943
2: Carabiniere, Italian Carabinieri
   Reali, 1940
3: Greek ELAS partisan, 1944

H

11th Macedonia, 13th Roumelia and 16th Thessaly: the last two subsequently being amalgamated). These were lightly-armed formations of 3,000 to 6,000 men each.

ELAS's main rival was the constitutionalist EDES (the National Republican Greek League). This was smaller and largely restricted to Epirus, but because it received rather more British aid (and also some covert German assistance) it was better armed and more conventional in structure.

Both organisations devoted more attention to opposing each other than to fighting the Germans. The British negotiated a 'National Bands Agreement' in mid-1943, but open fighting broke out between ELAS and EDES in October, and again in early 1944. The British tried to patch up the quarrel at the Lebanon conference of mid-1944, but ELAS refused to join the proposed 'National Army', and gathered its strength for a final confrontation with the constitutionalists after the Germans had left.

In the meantime, the Germans were faced with the problems caused by the Italian defection and the increased possibility of an Allied landing. They succeeded in disarming the Italian garrisons, and even conducted a successful amphibious campaign in the Aegean in August 1944, but they were seriously short of security troops for the mainland. They extended the Bulgarian occupation area, and raised an experimental battalion of Greek volunteers. This proved so successful that by mid-1944 there were 15,000 Greeks (anti-Communists rather than pro-Germans) in 30 Security Bns. administered by the collaborationist Rallis government.

By late 1944 the Germans were beginning to withdraw from Greece, leaving arms behind in the hope that the guerillas would fight each other over them rather than harass the German retreat, as in fact happened. The British and royalist Greek forces landed in the south and quickly found themselves fighting ELAS, in what came to be called the 'Second Round' of the Greek Civil War (the 'First Round' being the fighting during the German occupation). EDES was defeated in the mountains, and its members were evacuated by British ships. The Security Bns. melted away, to re-appear from November 1944 onwards in the guise of constitutionalist National Guard battalions. There were to be 35 of these, with another three on Crete. Helped by the British, the constitutionalist forces

were able to defeat ELAS and force its hard core members over the border into Communist Albania, where they prepared for the 'Third Round'. The Greek Civil War was still far from over.

Albania

On Good Friday, 7 April 1939, an Italian Expeditionary Corps invaded Albania and within a week had occupied the country. After brief initial resistance the 10,000-strong Royal Albanian Army disintegrated. King Zog fled to exile and obscurity in London, and the Italian King Vittorio Emmanuele III usurped the Albanian throne.

The unsuccessful attempt of Abas Kupi, a royal official, to start a rebellion in Durrës was followed by two years of relative calm, with an Italian

Pavelić in a typically sinister pose, dressed rather incongruously as a Moslem member of the notorious 'Black Legion', probably as a gesture of solidarity between the Catholic Croats and Moslem Bosnians.

garrison consisting of the 'Puglie', 'Firenze', 'Parma' and 'Arezzo' Divisions. An Albanian Royal Guard was based in Rome, and four Albanian Fascist Militia Legions (1st to 4th) were established, wearing white fezzes and Italian MVSN uniform. An indigenous Police Force was formed, and Albanians were admitted to the Italian Navy, Air Force, Frontier Guard, Customs Guard and Carabinieri. Six Royal Albanian infantry battalions and three artillery batteries became attached to Italian units; and these, plus two new light anti-aircraft batteries, five irregular Volunteer Battalions and the 1st and 2nd Legions, performed disastrously in the 1940 Greek campaign. Nevertheless, in 1941 Greek Southern Epirus and Yugoslav Kosovo and Western Macedonia, each with Albanian majority populations, were ceded to Albania.

July 1943: German Police troops, accompanied by what appear to be members of the Serbian Volunteer Corps, on anti-partisan duty in Yugoslavia. The local farm cart seems to have been pressed into service to carry their heavy weapons. (Courtesy Brian L. Davis)

With an increase in guerilla activity the 1st to 3rd Albanian Rifle Regts. (Cacciatori d'Albania) were formed in late 1941, each 2,300 strong, with two infantry battalions, a machine gun company and a four-gun artillery battery. In spring 1943 the 4th Regt. was raised in Kosovo, and joined the 1st in the 1st Albanian Rifle Bde., but unreliability and desertions forced the 2nd and 3rd Regts. to disband just before the Italian Armistice.

The Albanian Communist Party under Enver Hoxha was based in Southern Albania, and after June 1941 small independent detachments began to ambush Italian patrols. In spring 1942 mobile battalions and local village militias were formed, and in April 1943 a British Military Mission to the Albanian Resistance arrived, favouring especially the Partisans. In May Operational Zones and a General Staff were established, and by July the 20 battalions and 30 detachments, totalling 10,000 men, were christened the National Liberation Army under General (Gjeneral-Kolonel) Enver Hoxha. Hoxha tried to unite all Albanian guerillas

in a 'National Freedom Movement' through the Mukaj Pact, but this strategy soon collapsed when it was recognised as a ploy to extend Communist influence to Northern Albania. In August 1943 the 1st Shock Bde., organised on the Yugoslav pattern with five battalions and an artillery battery, was formed.

Other Albanian forces were less well organised. In the North local clans continued their traditional Balkan guerilla warfare. In Central Albania around Krujë the redoubtable Abas Kupi, who had returned from Yugoslavia in April 1941, attempted to re-establish guerilla operations notwithstanding the unreliability of his men and the loss of the Yugoslav sanctuary after the German occupation of Yugoslavia. In the South conservative anti-Communist, anti-royalist politicians set up 'Balli Kombëtar' (named after its founder) in late 1942. A few weak 'battalions' were formed, but fear of Italian reprisals against civilians made them reluctant to fight aggressively.

The Italian Armistice of September 1943 was the turning-point of the war in Albania. Some Italian troops fled to Yugoslavia; but the entire 'Firenze' Div. joined the Partisans, supplying 1st Shock Bde. with the 'Antonio Gramsci Bn.' (later 'Bde'), some 1,500 strong. The Germans rushed 21st Mountain Corps (100th Jäger and 297th Infantry Divs.) to Albania, but otherwise were content to leave the running of the country to an Albanian National Committee. This Committee promptly severed all ties with Italy, and attempted to extricate itself from its inevitable association with the Germans by unilaterally declaring Albania a neutral country, citing the equivalent position of Egypt, which was recognised as neutral in spite of Allied occupation. In spite of such legalisms, however, the war continued. By early 1944 Albanian collaborationist forces included the 1st and 4th Rifle Regts., four Fascist Militia battalions, and the Gendarmerie, formed in spring 1943 under Gen. Prenk Previsi. In April 1944 in Kosovo 6,500 Albanians were formed into the (largely notional) SS-Mountain Division 'Skanderbeg', but it performed poorly against the Partisans before final disbandment in October.

Following the collapse of the Mukaj Pact in late 1943 relations between the guerilla factions degenerated into armed conflict. Abas Kupi returned to Krujë and in December formed the royalist,

Lieutenants Miloš Vonjnovic, commander of the 4th Regiment of the Serbian Volunteer Corps (left), and Vladimir-Vlada Lenac, both wearing Royal Yugoslav Army uniform carried over into the Corps.

mainly Moslem, 'Legaliteti' movement (often called the 'Zogists'), and continued his sporadic raiding. Balli Kombëtar, however, preferred German rule to Italian and, believing that only the Germans would allow Kosovo to remain Albanian after the war, began to collaborate. By early 1944, 20 of their battalions were fighting the Partisans alongside German units.

In December 1943 the Germans attacked Partisan areas in Southern Albania, but Hoxha's forces, now 35,000 men in the 1st to 6th Bdes., withdrew into the mountains. In February 1944 they re-emerged, re-occupied the south and began advancing northwards. In May the 1st Shock Div. (1st, 2nd, 5th Bdes.) was formed, as was the 'Anti-Fascist National Liberation Council', a provisional government dominated by Communists. Almost immediately German and Balli Kombëtar troops resumed the offensive in the south, driving the Partisans, including the new 7th to 12th Bdes., into Central Albania. There they fought more German units, including the 'Skanderbeg' Division. In July they annihilated the poorly-equipped Legaliteti forces, although Abas Kupi did escape to Italy. Then the 1st Div., supported by Yugoslav Partisans, attacked Gendarmerie units in Western Macedonia, forcing Previsi to seek sanctuary with the British Mission.

In August 1944 the 2nd Shock Div. was formed, and combined with the 1st in the 1st Army Corps. Hoxha now had 70,000 men in Brigades 1 to 22 (23

'Generallautnant' Shteyfon, Commander of the Russian Defence Corps, inspects his troops in Serbia, in 1943. Though no details can be seen, it is at least clear that all wear the regulation Germany Army uniform authorised for the Corps in December 1942.

and 24 were formed later) and territorial battalions. But Tirana remained in enemy hands, and so in October he sent 1st Div. (1st, 4th, 23rd Bdes.), and the 3rd, 6th, 8th and 10th Bdes., to take the city, a task accomplished after three weeks of heavy fighting. Meanwhile British troops were supporting the Partisans along the coast, and Balli Kombëtar was disintegrating as the Germans evacuated Albania. By December they had all gone. During 1945 four more divisions (3rd to 6th) were formed from existing brigades, and the 5th and 6th Divs. (seven brigades) were supporting Yugoslav Partisans in Kosovo.

* * *

The Plates

A1: Leutnant (2nd Lieutenant), Galician Police; Polish Government-General, 1942

The Ukrainians of the Galician Police wore a uniform of the same blue as the Polish Police, but markedly different in style. Instead of a peaked cap they had the Bergmütze, with the band cut away at the front in the traditional Ukrainian 'V', and a gold cockade with a blue trident, the traditional Ukrainian colours and symbol. The tunic had three-pointed pocket flaps instead of the square-cut Polish ones, and the cuffs were round instead of pointed. The zig-zag collar patch (plain for NCOs, silver-edged for officers) was deliberately based on that worn by the soldiers of the Western Ukrainian Republic of 1918–1920, though the rank devices were German in style. The 'GENERAL-GOUVERNEMENT' cuff band in red with silver lettering and green edging was worn by both Polish and Galician Police. Galicia also raised the 14th SS-Division and Galician SS-Police Regts. 4 to 7.

A2: Wachtmeister (Corporal), German Police Battalion, 1942

The German Police, who were unified in 1936, included the militarised Schutzpolizei, who were organised into mobile battalions (later regiments) equipped with infantry weapons and even light armour for an internal security role. The younger and fitter men were drafted into the Waffen-SS's 4th Polizei-Division in 1939, while others went to the new Police battalions set up to control the occupied territories. This NCO is in light field order. He wears the somewhat old-fashioned green uniform with its brown collar and cuffs, and has a field cap instead of the full dress shako or service dress peaked cap. In the field the Police wore standard steel helmets with the Police badge in silver on black on the left hand side. In 1943 the Police began to receive plain Wehrmacht-style tunics in the same shade of green. The Gendarmerie, or rural constabulary, wore similar uniforms with orange piping and sleeve badges.

A3: German SS-Untersturmführer (2nd Lieutenant), SD-Einsatzgruppe; Occupied Russia, 1941

The SD (Sicherheitsdienst, or Security Service) was the intelligence arm of the General SS and, under Himmler, controlled the police forces of both Germany and the occupied territories. The SD never formed part of the Waffen-SS. Its members were not just office warriors, however: they commanded the infamous Einsatzgruppen or extermination groups in Russia, and took part in many anti-partisan operations. The field grey uniform—shown here in the pre-war version with silver collar piping—was generally used during the war in preference to the old black one: both open and closed collars were worn. At first the SD used the same Army-style shoulder straps as the Waffen-SS, but the latter objected, and in January 1942 the SD adopted Police-style shoulder straps in silver and black. They were supposed to wear Police-green piping on the peaked-cap, but in practice many wore the white of the Allgemeine-SS. Note the SD's plain right hand collar patch.

B1: Virsseržants (Staff Sergeant), Latvian 'Schuma', 1941

When the Russians occupied the Baltic States in 1940 the Estonian, Latvian and Lithuanian armies were incorporated into the Red Army *en bloc*, still wearing their old uniforms with only the insignia changed. When the Germans came many of these men joined the 'Schuma'. The early Schuma were a heterogeneous collection of police, home guards and nationalist militias, with no standard uniform, and this Latvian regular NCO has simply restored the original insignia to his pre-war uniform. The cap badge is the crest from the national arms: the same device was later worn as a collar patch by Latvian Waffen-SS troops, in the same way as the white stripe on the collar patch re-appeared on the armshield. Patch and piping are in infantry crimson: artillery wore dark blue and cavalry, yellow. Officers had a tunic with six buttons and 'French' cuffs. Some Latvian Schuma wore Czech helmets instead of the German M16 model used before the war.

B2: Korporal (Corporal), Ukrainian 'Schuma', 1942

The need to provide uniforms for the motley collection of Schuma personnel became urgent during 1942, particularly since the Army's Eastern Battalions were already wearing field grey. The German Police collected unwanted black Allgemeine-SS uniforms and sent them east for distribution, although most Baltic ex-servicemen and policemen continued to wear their distinctive pre-1940 uniforms. The conspicuous black uniform was of course adequate for normal police duties. Regulations demanded that all SS insignia be removed and 'Police-green' (light green) lapels, shoulder straps, pocket flaps and deep cuffs be added—although this uniform lacks the straps. No cap badge was prescribed, but Ukrainians often wore the traditional trident badge, and Balts their old Army or Police cap-badges. Rank insignia was introduced in May 1942 and worn by NCOs on the lower left sleeve. A Schutzmann had no insignia; an Unterkorporal a silver braid bar; a Vizekorporal a silver braid chevron and bar; a Korporal a chevron and two bars; a Vizefeldwebel a chevron and three bars; a Kompaniefeldwebel a chevron and four bars. Officers wore normal German Police shoulder-straps: Zugführer (Leutnant in the Baltic Schuma), flat silver braids; Oberzugführer (Oberleutnant), with a gold pip; Kompanieführer (Hauptmann), two gold pips; Bataillonsführer (Major), twisted silver braids; Bataillonsführer mit dem Range eines Oberstleutnants (Oberstleutnant), with a gold pip.

B3: Korporal, Ukrainian 'Schuma' Battalion, 1943

As the war intensified the black Schuma uniform was considered too conspicuous, especially for battalions in the field. Therefore in 1942 field uniforms began to be issued, probably in German Army field-grey, although this figure is wearing the Army uniform in the greenish colour introduced in 1943 for all German Police units. At first the cap badge was an embroidered branch-colour swastika and wreath on a dark green background, while the sleeve badge was larger, and also incorporated the branch-colour motto 'TREU – TAPFER – GEHORSAM' ('Loyal – Brave – Obedient'). The dark green shoulder straps (for ranks below officer) were piped in branch-colour with an aluminium thread embroidered swastika. Branch-colours were light green for urban Einzeldienst, orange for rural Einzeldienst, and crimson for Feuerschutzmannschaft; corresponding to the colours worn by the German Urban Police (Schutzpolizei), Rural Police (Gendarmerie), and Fire Service (Feuerschutzpolizei). Later however a standard pattern Schuma insignia was issued for all branches, with branch-colour insignia being replaced by grey-green embroidery on a black background or strap. Officers continued to wear aluminium wire insignia in place of the branch-colour on cap and sleeve. The rank insignia introduced in May 1942 for Schuma was worn on this uniform, but this particular NCO, taken from a German Police photograph, is wearing collar-patch insignia for which no official documentary proof has yet emerged—although it, and those of other figures in the photograph, superficially resembles insignia worn by Army-sponsored Eastern Legions, Eastern Battalions, Protection Battalions and home guard units. A rank-chart of this insignia has been published, but since the only evidence is the one photograph the chart must remain unconfirmed. Indeed, it may be that the original insignia was unofficial and confined to one unit. (Erratum: the 'L' of braid should appear on both patches.)

Ukrainian Insurgent Army (UPA) insignia, introduced 26 January 1944. Tridents and Field Marshal's chevron gold, other officers' chevrons and stripes silver, NCOs' stripes red, all worn on lower left sleeve. The 'Strilets' (Private) wore no insignia.

C1: Partisan, Polish People's Army (AL), 1944

This partisan is interesting in that he displays all three types of insignia used by the left-wing guerilla groups. The Gwardia Ludowa's badge was a red triangle with the organisation's initials in white embroidery or brass metal, worn either as a cap or a sleeve badge. When the GL became the Armia Ludowa it simply altered the initials to 'AL' (it is interesting to note that the Polish Communists, unlike their East European comrades, carefully avoided using the red star). The AL also used the national white or silver eagle, though they removed

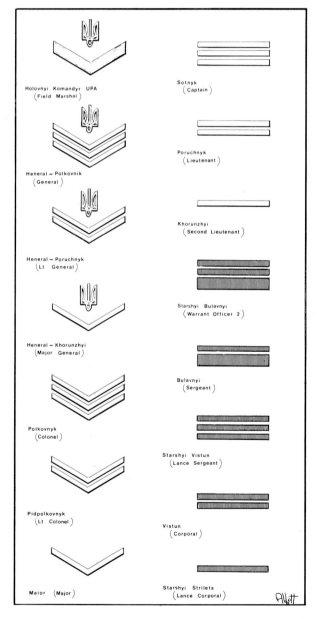

Holovnyi Komandyr UPA
(Field Marshal)

Heneral – Polkovnik
(General)

Heneral – Poruchnyk
(Lt General)

Heneral – Khorunzhyi
(Major General)

Polkovnyk
(Colonel)

Pidpolkovnyk
(Lt Colonel)

Maior (Major)

Sotnyk
(Captain)

Poruchnyk
(Lieutenant)

Khorunzhyi
(Second Lieutenant)

Starshyi Bulavnyi
(Warrant Officer 2)

Bulavnyi
(Sergeant)

Starshyi Vistun
(Lance Sergeant)

Vistun
(Corporal)

Starshyi Strilets
(Lance Corporal)

the crown and sometimes added 'AL' to the shield at the bottom. This partisan, obviously an early recruit, wears both the 'GL' badge and the 'AL' eagle: in addition he has an AL armband in the national colours. He wears a Wehrmacht tunic with the insignia removed: the rest of his clothing, including the beret, is civilian.

C2: Russian partisan, 1942

Communications between the 'Little Land', or partisan territory, and the 'Great Land', or unconquered Russia, were too tenuous to allow anything but the most essential supplies to be sent. Uniforms had a low priority, and the partisans had to fend for themselves; only occasionally were there deliveries of boots and special winter clothing. Some Red Army stragglers kept their uniforms, but many others threw them away during the first winter of the war, and the average partisan detachment was dressed in civilian clothes. Some of the peasant recruits wore the traditional high-collared shirt-blouse and peaked cap, but both Russian and German photographs show a preponderance of 'proletarian' clothing: baggy suit jackets and trousers, town shirts and the ubiquitous cloth cap. Insignia was conspicuous by its absence. This partisan has a pair of high boots, but is otherwise dressed as an urban worker. He carries the effective PPSh. 41 sub-machine gun.

C3: Partisan, Ukrainian Insurgent Army (UPA), 1943

This partisan is based on a drawing in a Ukrainian language source. He appears to be wearing an Italian Army tunic, which is by no means impossible as the UPA certainly obtained some arms from Italian troops in Russia. The breeches are of Russian origin, and the cap is probably of local manufacture. The 'V'-shaped indentation in the band was a traditional feature of Ukrainian military dress, and appeared in the *kappis* worn by the Galician Sich Rifles of the old Austro-Hungarian Empire. Photographs show that the UPA wore a variety of costumes, including captured German Police and old Polish uniforms, but the Wehrmacht's field grey tunic and peaked field cap seem to have been the most common. Insignia, if worn, took the form of the trident of Vladimir on a background of yellow and light blue, but rank devices were not introduced until 26 January 1944.

D1: Satnik (Captain), Black Legion of the Ustasha Militia; Croatia, 1942

Ustasha militiamen originally wore the Italian Colonial uniform of Ethiopian War vintage, but soon changed to the standard Italian Army grey-green. As Militia and Army units integrated later in the war, the German-style 1942 Croat Army

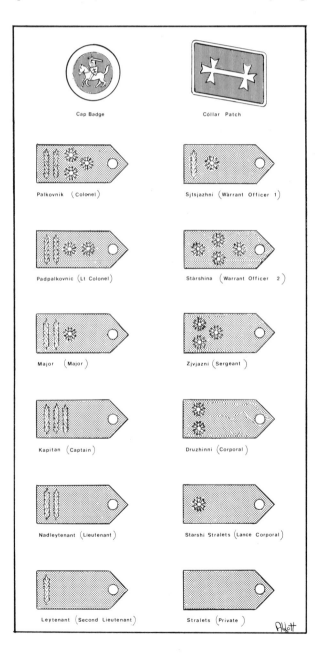

Cap Badge — Collar Patch

Palkovnik (Colonel) — Sjtsjazhni (Warrant Officer 1)

Padpalkovnic (Lt Colonel) — Stärshina (Warrant Officer 2)

Major (Major) — Zjvjazni (Sergeant)

Kapitan (Captain) — Druzhinni (Corporal)

Nadleytenant (Lieutenant) — Starshi Stralets (Lance Corporal)

Leytenant (Second Lieutenant) — Stralets (Private)

Byelorussian Home Guard (BKA) insignia, introduced early 1944. Cap and collar-badges red and white (the Byelorussian national colours). Rank devices yellow on field grey. The 'Stralets' (Private) wore no insignia.

Upper panel: **Croatian Army. NDH badge gold, cockade dark-blue and white with red centre; leaves gold (Generals) or silver (other officers). Collar-patches red (Generals and Artillery); black velvet with red stripe (General Staff); yellow (Cavalry); crimson (Infantry); green (Engineers); black (Medical). Field Marshal's collar devices gold rosettes on silver lace; other Generals silver devices on gold lace; Field Officers gold devices on silver lace; Company Officers silver devices and braid (the 'Nadsatnik'—Senior Captain, wore a Captain's insignia in gold); 'Zastavnik' and 'Časnički Namjesnik' silver devices and braid; other NCOs white devices and silver braid.**
Lower panel: **Ustasha Militia. Badge silver, shield silver and red. All rank devices red, officers' devices worn on both cuffs and side-cap. NCOs' devices on upper left sleeve only. The 'Vojnicar' (Private) wore no insignia.**

uniform became more common. Steel helmets could be German or Italian, and sometimes bore a white painted 'U' on the front. As a member of the élite 1st Ustasha Regt. (usually, but unofficially, called the Crna Legija—'Black Legion'), this officer wears a black uniform clearly modelled on the Italian Fascist Militia. In the field a black or grey-green Italian *bustina* side-cap was worn, with the Ustasha badge ('U' with grenade) on the front. Officers wore a small tricolour national cockade above. On the collar the Ustasha badge was worn,

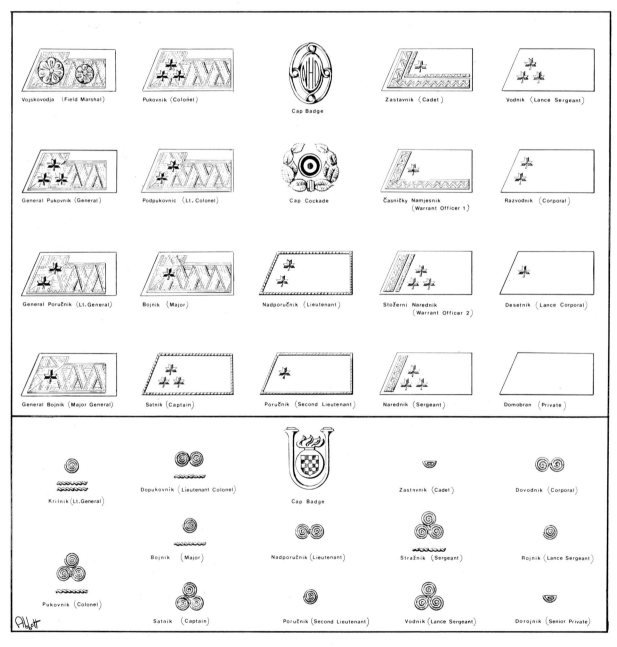

Upper panel (Croatian Army):

Vojskovodja (Field Marshal)	Pukovnik (Colonel)	Cap Badge	Zastavnik (Cadet)	Vodnik (Lance Sergeant)
General Pukovnik (General)	Podpukovnic (Lt. Colonel)	Cap Cockade	Časnički Namjesnik (Warrant Officer 1)	Razvodnik (Corporal)
General Poručnik (Lt. General)	Bojnik (Major)	Nadporučnik (Lieutenant)	Stožerni Narednik (Warrant Officer 2)	Desetnik (Lance Corporal)
General Bojnik (Major General)	Satnik (Captain)	Poručnik (Second Lieutenant)	Narednik (Sergeant)	Domobran (Private)

Lower panel (Ustasha Militia):

Krilnik (Lt. General)	Dopukovnik (Lieutenant Colonel)	Cap Badge	Zastavnik (Cadet)	Dovodnik (Corporal)
	Bojnik (Major)	Nadporučnik (Lieutenant)	Stražnik (Sergeant)	Rojnik (Lance Sergeant)
Pukovnik (Colonel)	Satnik (Captain)	Poručnik (Second Lieutenant)	Vodnik (Lance Sergeant)	Dorojnik (Senior Private)

Abbott

sometimes on a red, or on a red, white and dark blue striped collar-patch. Officers wore the distinctive and elegant red embroidered rank insignia on both cuffs and on the left side of the side-cap, while NCOs only wore it on the left upper arm.

The 'Black Legion' was formed by Jure Francetić in Sarajevo in September 1941, and immediately gained a fearsome reputation as an effective anti-partisan unit fighting Partisans and Chetniks in Bosnia. So excessive, and ultimately counter-productive were its atrocities, that the Germans demanded it be disbanded; but Pavelić refused, and defiantly appointed Francetić to the number two Ustasha post of commander of Ustasha field units. In January 1943 Francetić fell in action, and the Legion was indeed broken up, with most legion-naires going to form the 1st Mobile Brigade. All former members of the Legion wore the black uniform until the end of the war.

D2: Visji Narednik (Staff Sergeant), Slovene Home Guard, 1944

The Slovene Home Guard was formed from Slovenes who had collaborated with the Italians during their occupation. It is not clear what they wore during the earlier period, but in the later stages of the war they were issued with German uniforms which they wore with their own rank insignia. A general had twisted gold shoulder cords of the Yugoslav pattern and with the same blue-grey backing; senior officers, plain gold, and junior officers plain silver shoulder boards, made of a smooth plastic-like material and worn with one to three Yugoslav-style rank stars. NCOs, however, wore straps edged with silver braid after the German fashion, but with Russian-style transverse bars, also in silver. The white shield and blue eagle of the sleeve badge recall that the Slovene col-laborationist forces were known to the Partisans as 'White Guards' and 'Blue Guards'.

D3: Narednik (Sergeant) of Croatian infantry, 1943

The Croatian Army began by wearing Yugoslav uniforms with modified insignia, but in 1942 it introduced its own design. This was German in style, field-grey in colour, and with a conventional tunic. Officers had a peaked cap with a wreathed national cockade surmounted by an oval badge with the initials 'NDH' ('Independent State of

A German general is entertained by a Bulgarian lieutenant-general (left), who wears his collar-patches upside-down, and a Bulgarian staff officer displaying the First World War pilot's brevet on his left chest.

Croatia' in Croat), the whole arrangement clearly inspired by the German eagle and cockade. How-ever the rank insignia continued the pre-1918 Austro-Hungarian tradition (Croatia had formed part of Hungary until the end of the First World War, and the Hungarian 42nd Division had been formed from Croat conscripts and christened 'Croatian Defence Army', before the collapse of the Austro-Hungarian Empire). The Austrian star was replaced by the distinctive Croatian trefoil, and all ranks wore what was really the old Austrian *kappi* headgear, in 1943 adopted and modified by the Germans as the Einheitsmütze. The *kappi* was frequently worn by Croatian Legion units, which otherwise wore German uniforms with red and white chequered armshields.

A youthful member of Greek 'ELAS', in 1944, wearing British-supplied uniform items, and on his distinctive cap a crudely manufactured cockade and ELAS initials.

E1: Kapetan I Klase (Senior Captain), Serbian State Guard, 1941

The Serbian State Guard wore the old Yugoslav army uniform, large stocks of which were available in store after the Yugoslav surrender. The shoulder boards were basically Russian in style, but commonly employed gilt metal or plastic bars instead of braid, and the Yugoslav Army 'pips' resembled the German pattern. This uniform was really the old Serbian one dating from before the First World War, and its continued use illustrated the extent to which the Serbs had dominated the new state and its army. Up to 1940 officers wore a green-grey uniform, while men used a greyish ochre shade and had double-breasted tunics; but in that year a new universal uniform began to be introduced. The tunic remained similar to the old officer's pattern, single-breasted with a fly front and 'Austrian' pattern three-pointed pocket flaps, but the colour was more of an olive green. Officers and NCOs now wore peaked caps for dress, though all ranks continued to wear the old Serb cap for service.

E2: Kaplar (Lance Corporal), Serbian Volunteer Corps, 1942

The right-wing Volunteer Corps was strongly anti-Communist and, though small, provided the most effective anti-partisan force available to the collaborationist Serbian government. Its members wore the Yugoslav Mountain Troops' uniform, which differed from the standard model in that the tunic had six visible buttons, a turn-down collar and patch pockets. These retained the traditional three-pointed flaps, and the uniform as a whole kept the same general outline as before, with breeches, puttees and the traditional Serbian field cap. The Volunteers Corps' facings were blue. The cap badge was the double-headed Yugoslav eagle adopted by officers and NCOs in 1940 in place of the old oval cockade (curiously, the crown seems to have been retained even though the king was leading a government-in-exile). Rank insignia was the same as for the Yugoslav Army, with NCOs and men wearing dark blue straps. Like the State Guard, the Volunteers used the Czech M34 steel helmet.

E3: Kapitan (Captain), Russian Defence Corps, 1942

This corps was made up of White Russian exiles living in Yugoslavia. Many had seen service in the

Imperial Army, and jealously maintained their right to the traditional epaulettes. Consequently, while the collar patch showed the wearer's actual rank within the Corps, the shoulder strap showed his old Tsarist rank. Both were makeshift devices made up from uniform cloth and surplus Yugoslav rank stars. This Captain had served in the Imperial Army as an ensign. The uniform itself was originally made from Yugoslav khaki material; when this became unobtainable it was made from the brown cloth shown here. The service dress headgear was a peaked cap with the Imperial Russian cockade on

the front. At the end of 1942 the Corps was incorporated into the German Army and officially adopted the Wehrmacht's field grey, though in practice the old uniforms continued to be worn for some time. In 1945 members were ordered to wear Russian Army of Liberation armshields.

F1: Albanian Partisan, 1944

This figure is very much the Albanian partisan of post-war propaganda. In fact, like most guerillas, he is wearing a mixture of civilian clothing and captured enemy uniform. The khaki shirt is of uncertain origin, but the breeches are made from Italian 'grigio verde' material, and are worn with stockings and ankle-socks in the Italian fashion. The cap is clearly the Italian M1942, which was made with a fixed cloth peak. The rifle is Italian, too, though the bandolier is characteristically Balkan. The red scarf and star proclaim his political allegiance. In general, the Communist partisans seem to have worn conventional 'Proletarian' clothing, while the Constitutionalists were more likely to retain the striking Albanian regional costume. Both groups used captured uniforms, usually Italian, and later received British battle-dress, while some Communists had uniforms and rank insignia like those of the Yugoslav Partisans.

F2: Yugoslav Chetnik officer, 1943

This Chetnik commander wears what appears to be a version of the Mountain Troops' uniform, with its six visible buttons and practical turn-down collar. The 'spearhead' collar patch was more usually worn on the greatcoat collar. The black tasselled fez was worn by many Chetniks, though the style varied considerably. Others wore a low cylindrical black kalpak, sometimes with a red top, or else the old Serbian field cap. The black Chetnik banner bore a white skull and crossbones, and the same device was sometimes worn in silver on the uniform, but this officer's badge is the double-headed eagle cap badge of the Royal Army, as befits a member of

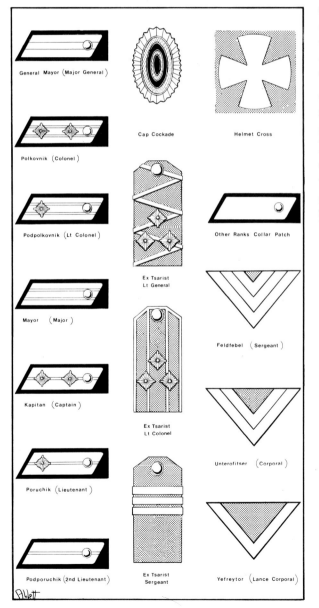

Russian Defence Corps (Serbia) insignia. Cockade orange-black-silver. Cross white. Collar-patches red (infantry); yellow (cavalry); light-blue (Cossacks). Major-General gold stripe, other officers silver stripes and pips, NCOs chevrons silver. Generals' shoulder-boards braided gold, other officers in branch colour, Senior NCOs thick stripes gold lace or yellow cloth, other NCOs thin stripes white cloth, all on brown or khaki base. The 'Strelok' (Private) or 'Kazak' (Cossack Private) wore no insignia.

the 'Yugoslav Army of the Homeland'. Many Chetniks followed the example of their leader Draža Mihailović and let their beards grow long as a sign that they were mourning the loss of Serbian freedom.

Yugoslav Partisan insignia:
Upper panel: **June 1941 to December 1942. All devices red, worn on left upper sleeve. Commissars wore similar devices but with white hammer and sickle on star. The 'Borac' (Private) wore no insignia.**
Centre panel: **December 1942 to April 1943. All devices red, worn on left upper sleeve. Commissars wore old devices. No insignia for 'Borac'.**
Lower panel: **May 1943 onwards. Officers' devices gold, WOs' and NCOs' white, worn on both cuffs. The 'Vojnik' (Private) wore 1–3 gold bars, with 1–3 white stars on the lower bar.**

F3: Kapetan (Captain), Yugoslav National Liberation Army, 1944
Tito and his staff evolved the workmanlike uniform shown here early in the war. The practical and comfortable tunic, with its turn-down collar and four outisde pockets, may have been inspired by the dress of the Royal Army's Mountain Troops. Tito himself introduced the Russian forage cap in place of the old Serbian model: known as a 'Titovka', this subsequently became regulation. Tito had been presented with an enamelled Red Army star with its hammer and sickle device, and his example was

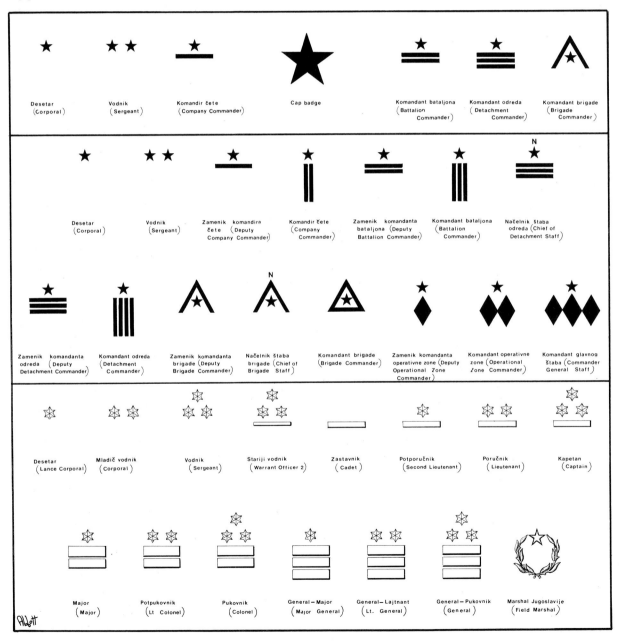

36

copied by the élite 'Proletarian' units, but most wore plain stars of red cloth. By 1943 Tito, something of a dandy, had a special dark grey Marshal's uniform with gold stars on the sleeves. The average Partisan was less well attired. In the beginning he wore a mixture of civilian clothing and old Royal Army uniform, later supplemented by captured German and Italian uniforms. From 1944 quantities of British battledress began to arrive from Italy: the Partisans wore these with their own field caps.

A rather dejected group of Albanian Partisans pose in a variety of uniform items of German, Italian and civilian origin. Note the red star worn by some of the men on their caps.

G1: Podofitser (Sergeant), Bulgarian Infantry, 1941

The Bulgarian occupation forces were made up largely of reservists, and the line divisions of the field army remained on the Turkish frontier until 1944. This NCO wears the standard brownish khaki winter service uniform with infantry collar patches and shoulder boards (the latter were supposed to be replaced by khaki ones, but photographs show that the coloured version continued to be worn throughout the war, presumably by reservists in the main). The field cap is reminiscent of the Italian model, a reminder that Italy and Bulgaria did indeed have ties in the inter-war period. It sometimes bore a gold rampant lion on the front. The tunic was practical and comfortable: some troops still wore the earlier model with a low standing collar and inset pockets with the same three-pointed flaps. There was also a peaked service dress cap with national cockade and branch colour band.

G2: Ushtar (Private), Albanian Rifles, 1942

When the Italians occupied Albania they incorporated the Albanian Army (which already had Italian instructors and equipment) into their own. The Royal Guard were outfitted with picturesque ceremonial uniforms based on Albanian folk dress, but the line battalions were put into the ordinary Italian 'grigio verde', and wore the collar patches of the Italian divisions to which they were attached. The only national distinction was the 'Skanderbeg helmet' (an antelope-crested helm worn by the medieval Albanian hero) above the five-pointed Italian collar star. When the Albanian troops were re-organised into separate rifle regiments in 1942 a new collar patch was introduced. The black and red stood for Albania, and the Savoy blue edging for the

Italian royal house. The Albanians re-asserted their independence after the Italian surrender of 1943, but it is not known whether any alterations were made to uniforms or insignia: given the chaotic political situation at the time, this seems unlikely.

G3: Podporuchik (2nd Lieutenant), Bulgarian Cavalry, 1942

Bulgarian officers wore a uniform which was similar to those of their men in style, but made of a more greenish shade of khaki. This officer wears the summer tunic of light greenish khaki linen: his men would have had a Russian-style shirt-blouse of the same material. It lacks the winter tunic's collar patch, which for cavalry would have taken the form of silver guard stripes with red piping. The steel helmet is the M1938, similar to the M1936, with the same semi-circular crown, but lacking the slight frontal crest of the earlier model. The same white-green-red shield that appeared on the field cap was worn on the right hand side. The officer's service dress cap had a black peak and a dark green band with arm-of-service piping. The oval cockade, often rendered incorrectly, had a red centre, a green ring, a red band, another green ring, and finally a broad white or silver outer band.

H1: Ypostrafigos (Major-General), Greek Security Battalions, 1943

This officer wears the same service dress that the Greek Army used in 1940–41, the only difference lying in the insignia. The circular blue and white cockade surmounted by a crown has been replaced

Enver Hoxha, political and military commander of the Albanian Partisans, and to date still virtually unchallenged ruler of Albania, wearing a uniform made up of captured Italian items, with a side-cap probably of Yugoslav Partisan origin.

by one bearing the Greek cross in white. This insignia probably dated from the period of the 1923–1935 Greek Republic. The crown has also been removed from the shoulder straps. This still allowed ranks to be distinguished, as generals wore gilt swords and batons over a large six-pointed silver star, field officers gold six-pointed stars, and company officers silver ones. NCOs and men also wore the old Greek army uniform, but some at least used the German steel helmet. Some of the Security Battalions were composed of Evzones, wearing their characteristic 'fustanella' or pleated skirt, with fez, khaki overjacket, tights and shoes decorated with woollen pompoms.

H2: Carabiniere, Italian Carabinieri Reali, 1940
The Carabinieri, like the French Gendarmerie, were a part of the armed forces, an élite para-military police force expected to defend the country in time of war as well as maintain order in peacetime. Founded in 1814, they had a long and honourable tradition. They acted as the Italian Army's military police wherever it served, and were inevitably involved in security matters. This mounted carabiniere wears the traditional *lucerna* or tricorne, with a green-grey cover and without the full dress plume of red over Savoy blue. It was usually replaced by the ordinary field cap in service. The cap badge consisted of grenade-like flames over the interlinked initials 'VE'. Obscured here are the black collar facings of the pre-1940 tunic with the traditional silver 'guard' stripes and the Italian Army's five-pointed active service star. The bandolier, in green-grey leather, was standard equipment for Italian mounted troops.

H3: Greek ELAS partisan, 1944
This mountaineer has followed Balkan guerilla custom and cultivated a ferocious beard. He wears a typical combination of local and orthodox military clothing. Guerilla forces throughout the Balkans generally began by wearing their own army uniforms. The Italian surrender of 1943 provided large quantities of 'grigio verde', but by 1944 these had to be supplemented by the hard-wearing and warm British battledress, which began to arrive in increasing quantities. This partisan has retained his old Greek Army tunic. He wears the typical mountaineer's goats'-hair cloak and a low fez, and

only a badge would indicate that he is ELAS rather than EDES. EDES was initially republican in sympathy and tended to wear Greek Army uniform with the crown removed, but later it moved towards the right and re-introduced the crown. The arrival of the British in 1944 encouraged the formation of a Royalist militia which wore orange armbands. ELAS seems to have worn a variety of locally made devices, usually incorporating its initials with either a Greek cross or a five-pointed star.

Albanian Partisans march in solemn triumph through the streets of liberated Tirana in November 1944. Note the cuff rank insignia worn by the second lieutenant (left foreground), clearly inspired by the Yugoslav model.

Notes sur les planches en couleur

A1 Les ukrainiens de la police galicienne portaient les emblèmes ukréniens traditionnels sur le calot et le col. Ils partageaient la couleur de l'uniforme et le brassard rouge, vert et argent avec la police polonaise. **A2** Un sous-officier d'un bataillon de *Schutzpolizei* en tenue de service de campagne dans les territoires occupés. **A3** La tunique d'officier SS d'avant-guerre avec col gris à passepoil argent portée ouverte à la discrétion personnelle. Une patte de col à droite noire et le losange de manche marqué 'SD' identifie la branche du service. Les épaulettes du style armée furent converties en style police en 1942.

B1 Uniforme et insigne d'avant-guerre de l'armée Lettone souvent portés par le personnel *Schuma* depuis les premiers jours chaotiques de l'organisation. **B2** Uniforme *Allgemeine-SS* noir de surplus avec distinction vert-police: les insignes de calot des anciennes organisations baltes—armée ou police—étaient souvent portés. **B3** L'année suivante, des uniformes gris ont été adoptés pour les unités en campagne puisqu'ils étaient moins voyants en opération. L'insigne de col, pris d'une photo, est inexpliqué.

C1 Ecusson de calot 'GL' triangulaire, rouge, porté à côté de l'insigne de l'aigle national, couronne enlevée; et (plus tard) un brassard 'AL'. A part la vieille tunique allemande, le costume est civil. **C2** Hormis les bottes de l'armée rouge, ce partisan porte une tenue civile de travailleur urbain. **C3** Une photo représente cette combinaison de casquette confection locale—noter la forme en V ukrainienne traditionnelle à l'avant—avec une vieille tunique italienne at des culottes de cheval russes.

D1 Uniforme modelé sur la milice fasciste italienne avec l'insigne de calot *Ustasha*, pattes de col bleu-blanc-rouge, avec 'U' noir, et insigne de grade rouge sur manche; ce dernier se trouve du côté gauche du calot. **D2** Uniforme allemand avec épaulettes Slovènes bordées et barrées d'argent en tant qu'insigne de grade, et insigne à aigle sur manche des forces collaboratrices Slovènes. **D3** Uniforme croatien de 1942 du style allemand mais conservant les éléments de l'insigne austro-hongrois d'avant 1918.

E1 Une forte influence serbe sur l'uniforme d'armée yougoslave d'avant 1941 l'a amenée à être conservé par les serbes avec la rédition. **E2** Uniforme de troupes de montagne yougoslaves d'avant 1941 avec parements bleus du corps de volontaires. Comme pour la garde d'état serbe, les casques tchèques de M34 étaient portés. **E3** Le grade russe tzariste ancien était porté sur les épaulettes et le rang actuel dans les cadres de cette organisation d'émigrés était porté sur le col.

F1 Les articles portés ici sont pour la plupart des butins de guerre pris aux Italiens. **F2** Cette organisation conservait notablement d'anciens uniformes d'armée yougoslave et des insignes, en l'occurrence ceux des troupes de montagne. Le *fez* noir en divers styles était en faveur; les barbes se portaient souvent longues. **F3** Tito et ses officiers d'Etat-Major portaient cet uniforme du début de la guerre, mais les humbles partisans se contentaient d'un lot hétéroclite d'articles yougoslaves, allemands, italiens et, plus tard, britanniques.

G1 Uniforme bulgare standard, avec insignes distinctives de l'infanterie sur le col et les épaulettes: ces dernières sont du type aux couleurs d'avant-guerre conservé par un grand nombré des réservistes ayant servi dans les troupes d'occupation. **G2** La tenue des officiers était d'un kaki à nuance plus verte; on voit ici la tunique d'été, sans insigne de col. Les hommes de troupe auraient porté une vareuse à la russe en tissu analogue. **G3** Uniforme foncièrement italien avec insigne nationale spéciale portée sur le col.

H1 Il s'agit de l'uniforme de base de l'armée grecque de 1940–41, les couronnes étant enlevées de la cocarde de casquette et des épaulettes et remplacées par une croix blanche sur la cocarde. **H2** Coiffe grise de service en campagne recouvrant la *lucerna* traditionnelle; on a ici une vue obscurcie des parements de col noirs de la tunique d'avant-guerre, portant la dentelle d'argent de la Garde et une étoile argent. **H3** Il s'agit fondamentalement de l'uniforme de l'armée grecque avec, en plus, la cape et le *fez*.

Farbtafeln

A1 Ukrainer in der galizischen Polizei trugen das traditionelle ukrainische Emblem auf Mütze und Kragen; ihre Uniform hatte dieselbe Farbe sowie die rot-grün-silberne Ambinde wie die polnische Polizei. **A2** Ein Unteroffizier vom Bataillon der *Schutzpolizei*; er trägt die Uniform für den Felddienst in den besetzten Gebieten. **A3** SS-Offiziersrock vor dem Krieg mit Silberkordel-Verzierung am grauen Kragen. Beachten Sie das schwarze Abzeichen auf dem rechten Kragen und das SD-Viereck auf dem Ärmel. Die Armee-Epauletten wurden 1942 durch Polizei-Epauletten ersetzt.

B1 Vorkriegsuniform und Insignien der Lettischen Armee, getragen von den *Schuma*-Mitgliedern, die im chaotischen Anfangsstadium der Organisation über eine Uniform verfügte. **B2** Schwarze *Allgemeine-SS*-Uniform mit polizeigrünen Auszeichnungen. Die Abzeichen auf den Mützen von früheren baltischen Organisationen, entweder Polizei oder Armee, wurden oft getragen. **B3** Im Jahr darauf wurden für die Feldeinheiten graue Uniformen eingeführt, die im Einsatz weniger auffällig waren. Die Insignien auf dem Kragen, die von einem Foto nachgebildet wurden, sind unbekannt.

C1 Das rote dreieckige GL-Mützenabzeichen wurde neben dem Adler ohne Krone getragen; mit Ausnahme des alten deutschen Waffenrocks ist dies eine zivile Ausstattung. **C2** Neben Stiefeln der Roten Armee trägt dieser Partisan die Zivilkleidung eines Stadtarbeiters. **C3** Auf dem Foto sehen Sie eine Kombination aus einer lokalen Mütze (beachten Sie vorn die traditionelle ukrainische Form des 'V'), eines alten italienischen Waffenrocks und russischen Kniehosen.

D1 Uniform nach dem Vorbild der Italienischen Faschistischen Miliz mit *Ustasha*-Mützenabzeichen, blau-weiss-rotem Kragenbesatz mit schwarzem 'U' und rotem Ranginsignien auf dem Ärmel. Letztere sind ebenfalls auf der linken Mützenseite zu sehen. **D2** Deutsche Uniform mit slovenischen, silber umrandeten Epauletten als Ranginsignien und dem Adler-Abzeichen der slovenischen Kollaborateure auf dem Ärmel. **D3** Kroatische Uniform aus dem Jahre 1942; vorwiegend deutscher Stil mit Elementen der österreich-ungarischen Insignien von der Zeit vor 1918.

E1 Der starke serbische Einfluss auf die Uniform der jugoslawischen Armee vor 1941 wurde nach der Kapitulation von den Serben beibehalten. **E2** Uniform der jugoslawischen Gebirgstruppen vor 1941 mit dem blauen Besatz des Freiwilligen-corps. Ebenso wie die Serbische Staatswache trug man tschechische M34-Helme. **E3** Auf den Epauletten trug man ehemalige zaristische russische Rangabzeichen und die gegenwärtigen Rangabzeichen dieser Organisation trug man auf dem Kragen.

F1 Hier trägt man vorwiegend erbeutete italienische Ausrüstung. **F2** Diese Organisation, nämlich die Gebirgstruppen, hat die ehemalige jugoslawische Armeeuniform grösstenteils übernommen. Sehr polulär war der schwarze *Fez* in verschiedenen Ausführungen; man trug oft lange Bärte. **F3** Tito und seine Stabsoffiziere trugen diese Uniform seit Kriegsbeginn, die briete Masse der Partisanen trug jedoch eine Mischung aus jugoslawischen, deutschen, italienischen und Britischen Kleidungsstücken.

G1 Bulgarische Standarduniform mit Infanterieauszeichnungen auf Kragen und Epauletten – letztere Auszeichnung mit den Vorkriegsfarben wurde von vielen Reservisten getragen, die als Besatzungstruppen dienten. **G2** Die Offiziere trugen eine etwas dunklere Farbe als khaki; dies ist der Waffenrock für den Sommer ohne Insignien auf dem Kragen. Gewöhnliche Soldaten trugen einen Kassak im russischen Stil aus demselben Material. **G3** Grundlegend italienische Uniform mit nationalen Insignien auf dem Kragen.

H1 Grundlegend griechische Armeeuniform aus dem Jahre 1940–41, jedoch ohne Krone getragen aus Mützenkrokarde und Epauletten. Die Krone auf der Krokarde wurde durch ein weisses Kreuz ersetzt. **H2** Traditionelle *Lucerna*-Mütze mit grauem Überzug für Feldeinsatz; nicht sehr deutlich erkennbar ist hier der schwarze Kragenbesatz auf dem Waffenrock von vor dem Krieg mit der Silberspitze der 'Wachen' und dem silbernen Stern. **H3** Grundlegend alte griechische Amreeuniform mit zusätzlichem Umhang und *Fez*.